# On Fear

Also by J.Krishnamurti

# On Fear

## J. Krishnamurti

## HarperOne

*An Imprint of* HarperCollins*Publishers*

HarperOne

For additional information, write to:
Krishnamurti Foundation Trust, Ltd.,
Brockwood Park, Bramdean, Hampshire, England S024 0LQ

or

Krishnamurti Foundation of America
P.O. Box 1560
Ojai, CA 93024–1560
U.S.A.

Sources and acknowledgments can be found on p. 121.

Series editor: Mary Cadogan

Associate editors: Ray McCoy and David Skitt

*Library of Congress Cataloging-in-Publication Data*

Krishnamurti, J. (Jiddu), 1895–1986
   On fear / J. Krishnamurti. — 1st ed.
     p. cm.
   ISBN: 978–0–06–251014–3
   1. Fear. I. Title.
B5134.K753K756   1994
128'.3—dc20                                                      94–19322

HB 07.25.2022

*There is fear. Fear is never an actuality; it is either before or after the active present. When there is fear in the active present, is it fear? It is there and there is no escape from it, no evasion possible. There, at that actual moment, there is total attention at the moment of danger, physical or psychological. When there is complete attention there is no fear. But the actual fact of inattention breeds fear; fear arises when there is an avoidance of the fact, a flight; then the very escape itself is fear.*

Krishnamurti's Notebook

# Contents

# Foreword

JIDDU KRISHNAMURTI was born in India in 1895 and, at the age of thirteen, was taken up by the Theosophical Society, which considered him to be the vehicle for the 'world teacher' whose advent it had been proclaiming. Krishnamurti was soon to emerge as a powerful, uncompromising, and unclassifiable teacher, whose talks and writings were not linked to any specific religion and were neither of the East nor the West but for the whole world. Firmly repudiating the messianic image, in 1929 he dramatically dissolved the large and monied organization that had been built around him and declared truth to be 'a pathless land,' which could not be approached by any formalized religion, philosophy, or sect.

For the rest of his life Krishnamurti insistently rejected the guru status that others tried to foist upon him. He continued to attract large audiences throughout the world but claimed no authority, wanted no disciples, and spoke always as one individual to another. At the core of his teaching was the realization that fundamental changes in society can be brought about only by a transformation of individual consciousness. The need for self-knowledge and understanding of the restrictive, separative influences of religious and nationalistic conditionings was constantly stressed. Krishnamurti pointed always to the urgent need for openness, for that 'vast space in the brain in which there is unimaginable energy'. This seems to have been the wellspring of his own creativity and the key to his catalytic impact on such a wide variety of people.

Krishnamurti continued to speak all over the world until he died in 1986 at the age of ninety. His talks and dialogues, journals and letters have been preserved in over sixty books and hundreds of recordings. From that vast body of teachings this series of theme books has been compiled. Each book focuses on an issue that has particular relevance to and urgency in our daily lives.

*On Fear*

# Bombay, 30 January 1982

We ARE GOING to talk over together the question of fear. But before we go into that I think we should learn the art of hearing. How to listen, not only to the speaker but to listen to those crows, listen to the noise, listen to your favourite music, listen to your wife or husband. Because we don't actually listen to people, we just casually listen and come to some kind of conclusion, or seek explanations, but we never actually listen to what somebody else is saying. We are always translating what others are saying. As we talk over together the very complex problem of fear, we aren't going to get trapped in too many details but will go into the whole movement of fear, and how we understand it, either verbally or actually. There is a difference between the comprehension of words and the comprehension of the actual state of fear. We are apt to make an abstraction of fear, that is, to make an idea of fear. But we never listen, apparently, to the voice of fear that is telling its story. And we are going together to talk about all that.

# Ojai, 8 May 1982

ONE ASKS WHY human beings, who have lived on this earth for million of years, who are technologically intelligent, have not applied their intelligence to be free from this very complex problem of fear, which may be one of the reasons for war, for killing one another. And religions throughout the world have not solved the problem; not the gurus, nor the saviours; nor ideals. So it is very clear that no outside agency—however elevated, however much made popular by propaganda—no outside agency can ever possibly solve this problem of human fear.

You are inquiring, you are investigating, you are delving into the whole problem of fear. And perhaps we have so accepted the pattern of fear that we don't want even to move away from it. So, what is fear? What are the contributory factors that bring about fear? Like many small streams, rivulets that make the tremendous volume of a river; what are the small streams that bring about fear? That have such tremendous vitality of fear. Is one of the causes of fear comparison? Comparing oneself with somebody else? Obviously it is. So, can you live a life comparing yourself with nobody? You understand what I am saying? When you compare yourself with another, ideologically, psychologically, or even physically, there is the striving to become that; and there is the fear that you may not. It is the desire to fulfil and you may not be able to fulfil. Where there is comparison there must be fear.

And so one asks whether it is possible to live without a single comparison, never comparing, whether you are beautiful or ugly, fair or not fair, approximating yourself to some ideal, to some pattern of values. There is this constant comparison going on. We are asking, is that one of the causes of fear? Obviously. And where there is comparison there must be conformity, there must be imitation. So we are saying that comparison, conformity, and imitation, are contributory causes of fear. Can one live without comparing, imitating, or conforming psychologically? Of course one can. If those are the contributory factors of fear, and you are concerned with the ending of fear, then inwardly there is no comparison, which means there is no becoming. The very meaning of the comparison is to become that which you think is better, higher, nobler, and so on. So, comparison is becoming. Is that one of the factors of fear? You have to discover it for yourself. Then if those are the factors, if the mind is seeing those factors as bringing about fear, the very perception of those ends the contributory causes. If there is a physical cause that gives you a stomachache, there is an ending of that pain by discovering the cause of it. Similarly, where there is any cause there is an ending.

# *From* Freedom from the Known

WHAT IS YOUR fundamental, lasting interest in life? Putting all oblique answers aside and dealing with this question directly and honestly, what would you answer? Do you know?

Isn't it yourself? Anyway, that is what most of us would say if we answered truthfully. I am interested in my progress, my job, my family, the little corner in which I live, in getting a better position for myself, more prestige, more power, more domination over others, and so on. I think it would be logical, wouldn't it, to admit to ourselves that that is what most of us are primarily interested in—me first?

Some of us would say that it is wrong to be primarily interested in ourselves. But what is wrong about it except that we seldom decently, honestly, admit it? If we do, we are rather ashamed of it. So there it is—one is fundamentally interested in oneself, and for various ideological or traditional reasons one thinks it is wrong. But what one thinks is irrelevant. Why introduce the factor of its being wrong? That is an idea, a concept. What is a fact is that one is fundamentally and lastingly interested in oneself.

You may say that it is more satisfactory to help another than to think about yourself. What is the difference? It is still self-concern. If it gives you greater satisfaction to help others, you are concerned with what will give you greater satisfaction. Why bring any ideological concept into it? Why this double thinking? Why not say, 'What I really want is satisfaction, whether in sex, or in helping others, or in becoming a great saint, scientist, or politician'? It is the same process, isn't it? Satisfaction, in all sorts of ways, subtle and obvious, is what we want. When we say we want freedom, we want it because we think it may be wonderfully satisfying, and the ultimate satisfaction, of course, is this peculiar idea of self-realization. What we are really seeking is a satisfaction in which there is no dissatisfaction at all.

Most of us crave the satisfaction of having a position in society because we are afraid of being nobody. Society is so constructed that a citizen who has a position of respect is treated with great courtesy, whereas a man who has no position is kicked around. Everyone in the world wants a position, whether in society, in the family, or to sit on the right hand of God, and this position must be recognized by others, otherwise it is no position at all. We must always sit on the platform. Inwardly we are whirlpools of misery and mischief and therefore, to be regarded outwardly as a great figure is very gratifying. This craving for position, for prestige, for power, to be recognized by society as being outstanding in some way, is a wish to dominate others, and this wish to dominate is a form of aggression. The saint who seeks a position in regard to his saintliness is as aggressive as the chicken pecking in the farmyard. And what is the cause of this aggressiveness? It is fear, isn't it?

Fear is one of the greatest problems in life. A mind that is caught in fear lives in confusion, in conflict, and therefore must be violent, distorted, and aggressive. It dare not move away from its own patterns of thinking, and this breeds hypocrisy. Until we are free from fear, we may climb the highest mountain, invent every kind of God, but we will remain in darkness.

Living in such a corrupt, stupid society as we do, with the competitive education we receive, which engenders fear, we are all burdened with fears of some kind, and fear is a dreadful thing that warps, twists, and dulls our days.

There is physical fear, but that is a response we have inherited from the animals. It is psychological fears we are concerned with here, for when we understand the deep-rooted psychological fears, we will be able to meet the animal fears, whereas to be concerned with the animal fears first will never help us to understand the psychological fears.

We are all afraid of something; there is no fear in abstraction, it is always in relation to something. Do you know your own fears—fear of losing your job, of not having enough food or money, or what your neighbours or the public think about you, or of not being a success, of losing your position in society, of being despised or ridiculed—fear of pain and disease, of domination, of never knowing what love is or of not being loved, of losing your wife or children, of death, of living in a world that is like death, of utter boredom, of not living up to the image others have built about you, of losing your faith—all these and innumerable other fears—do you know your own particular fears? And what do you usually do about them? You run away from them, don't you, or invent ideas and images to cover them? But to run away from fear is only to increase it.

One of the major causes of fear is that we do not want to face ourselves as we are. So, as well as the fears themselves, we have to examine the network of escapes we have developed to rid ourselves of them. If the mind, in which is included the brain, tries to overcome fear, to suppress it, discipline it, control it, translate it into terms of something else, there is friction, there is conflict, and that conflict is a waste of energy.

The first thing to ask ourselves then is what is fear and how does it arise? What do we mean by the word *fear* itself? I am asking myself what fear is, not what I am afraid of.

I lead a certain kind of life; I think in a certain pattern; I have certain beliefs and dogmas and I don't want those patterns of existence to be disturbed because I have my roots in them. I don't want them to be disturbed because the disturbance produces a state of unknowing and I dislike that. If I am torn away from everything I know and believe, I want to be reasonably certain of the state of things to which I am going. So the brain cells have created a pattern and those brain cells refuse to create another pattern, which may be uncertain. *The movement from certainty to uncertainty is what I call fear.*

At the actual moment, as I am sitting here, I am not afraid; I am not afraid in the present, nothing is happening to me, nobody is threatening me or taking anything away from me. But beyond the actual moment there is a deeper layer in the mind that is consciously or unconsciously thinking of what might happen in the future or worrying that something from the past may overtake me. So I am afraid of the past and the future. I have divided time into the past and the future. Thought steps in, says, 'Be careful it does not happen again', or 'Be prepared for the future. The future may be dangerous for you. You have got something now but you may lose it. You may die tomorrow, your wife may run away, you may lose your job. You may never become famous. You may be lonely. You want to be quite sure of tomorrow'.

Now take your own particular form of fear. Look at it. Watch your reactions to it. Can you look at it without any movement of escape, justification, condemnation or suppression? Can you look at that fear without the word that causes the fear? Can you look at death, for instance, without the word that arouses the fear of death? The word itself brings a tremor, doesn't it, as the word *love* has its own tremor, its own image? Now, is the image you have in your mind about death, the memory of so many deaths you have seen and the associating of yourself with those incidents—is it that image which is creating fear? Or are you actually afraid of coming to an end, not of the image creating the end? Is the word *death* causing you fear or the actual ending? If it is the word or the memory that is causing you fear then it is not fear at all.

You were ill two years ago, let us say, and the memory of that pain, that illness, remains, and the memory now functioning says, 'Be careful, don't get ill, again'. So the memory with its associations is creating fear, and that is not fear at all because at the moment you actually have very good health. Thought, which is always old, because thought is the response of memory and memories are always old—thought creates, in time, the feeling that you are afraid, which is not an actual fact. The actual fact is that you are well. But the experience, which has remained in the mind as a memory, rouses the thought, 'Be careful, don't fall ill again'.

So we see that thought engenders one kind of fear. But is there fear at all apart from that? Is fear always the result of thought and, if it is, is there any other form of fear? We are afraid of death—that is, something that is going to happen tomorrow or the day after tomorrow, in time. There is a distance between actuality and what will be. Now thought has experienced this state; by observing death it says, 'I am going to die'. Thought creates the fear of death, and if it doesn't, is there any fear at all?

Is fear the result of thought? If it is, thought being always old, fear is always old. As we have said, there is no new thought. If we recognize it, it is already old. So what we are afraid of is the repetition of the old—the thought of what has been projecting into the future. Therefore, thought is responsible for fear. This is so, you can see it for yourself. When you are confronted with something immediately there is no fear. It is only when thought comes in that there is fear.

Therefore, our question now is, is it possible for the mind to live completely, totally, in the present? It is only such a mind that has no fear. But to understand this, you have to understand the structure of thought, memory, and time. And in understanding it, understanding not intellectually, not verbally, but actually with your heart, your mind, your guts, you will be free from fear; then the mind can use thought without creating fear.

Thought, like memory, is, of course, necessary for daily living. It is the only instrument we have for communication, working at our jobs and so forth. Thought is the response to memory, memory that has been accumulated through experience, knowledge, tradition, time. And from this background of memory we react, and this reaction is thinking. So thought is essential at certain levels, but when thought projects itself psychologically as the future and the past, creating fear as well as pleasure, the mind is made dull and therefore inaction is inevitable.

So I ask myself, 'Why, why, why, do I think about the future and the past in terms of pleasure and pain, knowing that such thought creates fear? Isn't it possible for thought, psychologically, to stop, for otherwise fear will never end?'

One of the functions of thought is to be occupied all the time with something. Most of us want to have our minds continually occupied so that we are prevented from seeing ourselves as we actually are. We are afraid to be empty. We are afraid to look at our fears.

Consciously you can be aware of your fears, but at the deeper levels of your mind are you aware of them? And how are you going to find out the fears that are hidden, secret? Is fear to be divided into the conscious and the subconscious? This is a very important question. The specialist, the psychologist, and the analyst, have divided fear into deep or superficial layers, but if you follow what the psychologist says or what I say, you are understanding our theories, our dogmas, our knowledge; you are not understanding yourself. You cannot understand yourself according to Freud or Jung, or according to me. Other people's theories have no importance whatsoever. It is of yourself that you must ask the question, is fear to be divided into the conscious and subconscious? Or is there only fear, which you translate into different forms? There is only one desire; there is only desire. You desire. The objects of desire change, but desire is always the same. So perhaps in the same way there is only fear. You are afraid of all sorts of things but there is only one fear.

When you realize that fear cannot be divided you will see that you have put away altogether this problem of the subconscious and so have cheated the psychologists and the analysts. When you understand that fear is a single movement that expresses itself in different ways, and when you see the movement and not the object to which the movement goes, then you are facing an immense question: How can you look at it without the fragmentation that the mind has cultivated?

There is only total fear, but how can the mind, which thinks in fragments, observe this total picture? Can it? We have lived a life of fragmentation, and can look at that total fear only through the fragmentary process of thought. The whole process of the machinery of thinking is to break up everything into fragments: I love you and I hate you; you are my enemy, you are my friend; my peculiar idiosyncrasies and inclinations, my job, my position, my prestige, my wife, my child, my country and your country, my God and your God—all that is the fragmentation of thought. And this thought looks at the total state of fear, or tries to look at it, and reduces it to fragments. Therefore, we see that the mind can look at this total fear only when there is no movement of thought.

Can you watch fear without any conclusion, without any interference of the knowledge you have accumulated about it? If you cannot, then what you are watching is the past, not fear; if you can, then you are watching fear for the first time without the interference of the past.

You can watch only when the mind is very quiet, just as you can listen to what someone is saying only when your mind is not chattering with itself, carrying on a dialogue with itself about its own problems and anxieties. Can you in the same way look at your fear without trying to resolve it, without bringing in its opposite, courage—actually look at it and not try to escape from it? When you say, 'I must control it, I must get rid of it, I must understand it', you are trying to escape from it.

You can observe a cloud or a tree or the movement of a river with a fairly quiet mind because they are not very important to you, but to watch yourself is far more difficult because there the demands are so practical, the reactions so quick. So when you are directly in contact with fear or despair, loneliness or jealousy, or any other ugly state of mind, can you look at it so completely that your mind is quiet enough to see it?

Can the mind perceive fear and not the different forms of fear—perceive total fear, not what you are afraid of? If you look merely at the details of fear or try to deal with your fears one by one, you will never come to the central issue, which is to learn to live with fear.

To live with a living thing such as fear requires a mind and heart that are extraordinarily subtle, that have no conclusion and can therefore follow every movement of fear. Then, if you observe and live with it—and this doesn't take a whole day, it can take a minute or a second to know the whole nature of fear—if you live with it so completely you inevitably ask, 'Who is the entity who is living with fear? Who is it who is observing fear, watching all the movements of the various forms of fear as well as being aware of the central fact of fear? Is the observer a dead entity, a static being, who has accumulated a lot of knowledge and information about himself, and is it that dead thing who is observing and living with the movement of fear? Is the observer the past or is he a living thing?' What is your answer? Do not answer me, answer yourself. Are you, the observer, a dead entity watching a living thing or are you a living thing watching a living thing? Because in the observer the two states exist.

The observer is the censor who does not want fear; the observer is the totality of all his experiences about fear. So the observer is separate from that thing he calls fear; there is space between them; he is forever trying to overcome it or escape from it and hence this constant battle between himself and fear—this battle that is such a waste of energy.

As you watch, you learn that the observer is merely a bundle of ideas and memories without any validity or substance, but that fear is an actuality and that you are trying to understand a fact with an abstraction which, of course, you cannot do. But, in fact, is the observer who says 'I am afraid' any different from the thing observed, which is fear? The observer *is* fear and when that is realized there is no longer any dissipation of energy in the effort to get rid of fear, and the time-space interval between the observer and the observed disappears. When you see that you are a part of fear, not separate from it—that you are fear—then you cannot do anything about it; then fear comes totally to an end.

# Saanen, 22 July 1965

IS IT POSSIBLE to end all fear? One may be afraid of the dark, or of coming suddenly upon a snake, or of meeting some wild animal, or of falling over a precipice. It is natural and healthy to want to stay out of the way of an oncoming bus, for example, but there are many other forms of fear. That is why one has to go into this question of whether the idea is more important than the fact, the what is. If one looks at what is, at the fact, and not at the idea, one will see that it is only the idea, the concept of the future, of tomorrow, that is creating fear. It is not the fact that creates fear.

FOR A MIND burdened with fear, with conformity, with the thinker, there can be no understanding of that which may be called the original. And the mind demands to know what the original is. We have said it is God—but that again is a word invented by human beings in their fear, in their misery, in their desire to escape from life. When the human mind is free of all fear, then, in demanding to know what the original is, it is not seeking its own pleasure, or a means of escape, and therefore in that inquiry all authority ceases. Do you understand? The authority of the speaker, the authority of the church, the authority of opinion, of knowledge, of experience, of what people say—all that completely comes to an end, and there is no obedience. It is only such a mind that can find out for itself what the original is—find out, not as an individual mind, but as a total human being. There is no 'individual' mind at all—we are all totally related. Please understand this. The mind is not something separate; it is a total mind. We are all conforming, we are all afraid, we are all escaping. And to understand—not as an individual, but as a total human being—what the original is, one must understand the totality of man's misery, all the concepts, all the formulas that he has invented through the centuries. It is only when there is freedom from all this that you can find out whether there is an original something. Otherwise we are secondhand human beings; and because we are secondhand, counterfeit human beings, there is no ending to sorrow. So the ending of sorrow is in essence the beginning of the original. But the understanding that brings about the ending of sorrow is not just an understanding of your particular sorrow, or my particular sorrow, because your sorrow and my sorrow are related to the whole sorrow of mankind. This is not mere sentiment or emotionalism; it is an actual, brutal fact. When we understand the whole structure of sorrow and thereby bring about the ending of sorrow, there is then a possibility of coming upon that strange something that is the origin of all life—not in a test tube, as the scientist discovers it, but there is the coming into being of that strange energy that is always exploding. That energy has no movement in any direction, and therefore it explodes.

# Saanen, 21 July 1964

To understand fear, one has to go into the question of comparison. Why do we compare at all? In technical matters comparison reveals progress, which is relative. Fifty years ago there was no atomic bomb, there were no supersonic airplanes, but now we have these things; and in another fifty years we shall have something else that we don't have now. This is called progress, which is always comparative, relative, and our mind is caught in that way of thinking. Not only outside the skin, as it were, but also inside the skin, in the psychological structure of our own being, we think comparatively. We say, 'I am this, I have been that, and I shall be something more in the future'. This comparative thinking we call progress, evolution, and our whole behaviour—morally, ethically, religiously, in our business and social relationships—is based on it. We observe ourselves comparatively in relation to a society that is itself the outcome of this same comparative struggle.

Comparison breeds fear. Do observe this fact in yourself. I want to be a better writer, or a more beautiful and intelligent person. I want to have more knowledge than others; I want to be successful, to become somebody, to have more fame in the world. Success and fame are psychologically the very essence of comparison, through which we constantly breed fear. And comparison also gives rise to conflict, struggle, which is considered highly respectable. You say that you must be competitive in order to survive in this world, so you compare and compete in business, in the family, and in so-called religious matters. You must reach heaven and sit next to Jesus, or whoever your particular saviour may be. The comparative spirit is reflected in the priest becoming an archbishop, a cardinal, and finally the pope. We cultivate this same spirit very assiduously throughout our life, struggling to become better or to achieve a status higher than somebody else. Our social and moral structure is based on it.

So there is in our life this constant state of comparison, competition, and the everlasting struggle to be somebody—or to be nobody, which is the same thing. This, I feel, is the root of all fear, because it breeds envy, jealousy, hatred. Where there is hatred there is obviously no love, and fear is generated more and more.

# *From* The Impossible Question
## *Saanen, 3 August 1970*

WE ARE TALKING about fear, which is part of this total movement of the 'me'; the me that breaks up life as a movement, the me
that separates itself as the you and the me. We asked, 'What is fear?'
We are going to learn non-accumulatively about fear; the very word
*fear* prevents coming into contact with that feeling of danger that
we call fear. Look, maturity implies a total, natural development of
a human being; natural in the sense of non-contradictory, harmo-
nious, which has nothing to do with age. And the factor of fear prevents this natural, total development of the mind.

  When one is afraid, not only of physical things, but also of
psychological factors, what takes place in that fear? I am afraid,
not only of physically falling ill, of dying, of darkness—you know
the innumerable fears one has, both biological as well as psychological. What does that fear do to the mind, the mind that has created these fears? Do you understand my question? Don't answer
me immediately, look at yourselves. What is the effect of fear on
the mind, on one's whole life? Or are we so used to fear, have we
so accustomed ourselves to fear, which has become a habit, that
we are unaware of its effect? If I have accustomed myself to the
national feeling of the Hindu—to the dogma, to the beliefs—I
am enclosed in this conditioning and totally unaware of what the

effects of it are. I only see the feeling that is aroused in me, the nationalism, and I am satisfied with that. I identify myself with the country, with the belief and all the rest of it. But we don't see the effect of such a conditioning all around. In the same way, we don't see what fear does—psychosomatically, as well as psychologically. What does it do?

*Questioner:* I become involved in trying to stop this thing from happening.

*Krishnamurti:* It stops or immobilizes action. Is one aware of that? Are you? Don't generalize. We are discussing in order to see what is actually happening within us; otherwise this has no meaning. In talking over what fear does and becoming conscious of it, it might be possible to go beyond it. So if I am at all serious I must see the effects of fear. Do I know the effects of it? Or do I only know them verbally? Do I know them as something that has happened in the past, which remains a memory that says: 'These are the effects of it'? So that memory sees the effects of it, but the mind doesn't see the actual effect. I don't know if you see this? I have said something that is really quite important.

*Q:* Could you say it again?

*K:* When I say I know the effects of fear, what does that mean? Either I know it verbally, that is, intellectually, or I know it as a memory, as something that has happened in the past, and I say: 'This did happen'. So the past tells me what the effects are. But I don't see the effects of it at the actual moment. Therefore, it is something remembered and not real, whereas 'knowing' implies non-accumulative seeing—not recognition—but seeing the fact. Have I conveyed this?

When I say 'I am hungry', is it the remembrance of having been hungry yesterday that tells me, or is it the actual fact of hunger now? The actual awareness that I am hungry now is entirely different from the response of a memory that tells me I have been hungry and therefore I may be hungry now. Is the past telling you the effects of fear, or are you aware of the actual happening of the effects of fear? The actions of the two are entirely different, aren't they? The one, being completely aware of the effects of fear now, acts instantly. But if memory tells me these are the effects, then the action is different. Have I made myself clear? Now, which is it?

*Q:* Can you distinguish between a particular fear and actually being aware of the effects of fear as such—apart from remembering the effects of a fear?

*K:* That's what I was trying to explain. The action of the two are entirely different. Do you see that? Please, if you don't see it don't say 'yes', don't let's play games with each other. It is very important to understand this. Is the past telling you the effects of fear, or is there a direct perception or awareness of the effects of fear now? If the past is telling you the effects of fear, the action is incomplete and therefore contradictory; it brings conflict. But if one is completely aware of the effects of fear now, the action is total.

*Q:* As I am sitting in the tent now I have no fear because I am listening to what you are talking about, so I am not afraid. But this fear may come up as I leave the tent.

*K:* But can't you, sitting here in this tent, see fear, which you may have had yesterday? Can't you invoke it, invite it?

*Q:* It may be life fears.

*K:* Whatever the fear may be, need you say, 'I have no fears now, but when I go outside I'll have them'. They are there!

*Q:* You can invoke it—as you say—you can remember it. But this is the point you made about bringing in memory, the thought about fear.

*K:* I am asking: 'Need I wait until I leave the tent to find out what my fears are? Or, sitting here, can I be aware of them?' I am not afraid at this moment of what someone might say to me. But when I meet the man who is going to say these things, that will frighten me. Can't I see the actual fact of that now?

*Q:* If you do that, you are already making a practice of it.

*K:* No, it is not a practice. You see, you are so afraid of doing anything that might become a practice! Sir, aren't you afraid of losing your job? Aren't you afraid of death? Aren't you afraid of not being able to fulfil? Aren't you afraid of being lonely? Aren't you afraid of not being loved? Don't you have some form of fear?

*Q:* Only if there is a challenge.

*K:* But I am challenging you! I can't understand this mentality!

*Q:* If there is an impulse you act, you have to do something.

*K:* No! You are making it so complicated. It is as natural as hearing that train roar by. Either you can remember the noise of that train, or listen actually to that noise. Don't complicate it, please.

*Q:* Aren't you in a way complicating it by talking about invoking fear? I don't have to invoke any of my fears—just being here I can survey my reaction.

*K:* That's all I am saying.

*Q:* In order to communicate here we must know the difference between the brain and the mind.

*K:* We have discussed that before. We are now trying to find out what fear is, learn about it. Is the mind free to learn about fear? Learning being watching the movement of fear. You can only watch the movement of fear when you are not remembering past fears and watching with those memories. Do you see the difference? I can watch the movement. Are you learning about what is actually taking place when there is fear? We are boiling with fear all the time. We don't seem to be able to get rid of it. When you had fears in the past and were aware of them, what effect had those fears on you and on your environment? What happened? Weren't you cut off from others? Weren't the effects of those fears isolating you?

*Q:* It crippled me.

*K:* It made you feel desperate, you didn't know what to do. Now, when there was this isolation, what happened to action?

*Q:* It was fragmentary.

*K:* Do listen to this carefully, please. I have had fear in the past and the effects of those fears were to isolate me, to cripple me, to make me feel desperate. There was a feeling of running away, of seeking comfort in something. All that we will call for the moment isolating oneself from all relationship. The effect of that isolation in action is to bring about fragmentation. Didn't this happen to you? When you were frightened you didn't know what to do; you ran away from it, or tried to suppress it, or reason it away. And when you had to act you were acting from a fear that is in itself isolating. So an action born out of that fear must be fragmentary. Fragmentation being contradictory, there was a great deal of struggle, pain, anxiety, no?

*Q:* Sir, as a crippled person walks on crutches, so a person who is numbed, crippled by fear, uses various kinds of crutches.

*K:* That's what we are saying. That's right. Now you are very clear about the effect of past fear: it produces fragmentary actions. What is the difference between that and the action of fear without the response of memory? When you meet physical danger what takes place?

*Q:* Spontaneous action.

*K:* It is called spontaneous action—is it spontaneous? Please do inquire, we are trying to find out something. You are in the woods by yourself, in some wild part and suddenly you come upon a bear with cubs—what happens then? Knowing the bear is a dangerous animal what happens to you?

*Q:* The adrenalin is increased.

*K:* Yes, now what is the action that takes place?

*Q:* You see the danger of transmitting your own fear to the bear.

*K:* No, what happens to you? Of course if you are afraid you transmit it to the bear and the bear gets frightened and attacks you. Have you ever faced a bear in the woods?

*Q:* There is someone here who has.

*K:* I have. That gentleman and I have had many of these experiences during certain years. But what takes place? There is a bear a few feet away from you. There are all the bodily reactions, the flow of adrenalin, and so on; you stop instantly and you turn away and run. What has happened there? What was the response? A conditioned response, wasn't it? People have told you generation

after generation, 'Be careful of wild animals'. If you get frightened you will transmit that fear to the animal and then he will attack you. The whole thing is gone through instantly. Is that the
functioning of fear—or is it intelligence? What is operating? Is it
fear that has been aroused by the repetition of 'be careful of the
wild animals', which has been your conditioning from childhood?
Or is it intelligence? The conditioned response to that animal and
the action of that conditioned response is one thing. The operation of intelligence and the action of intelligence is different; the
two are entirely different. Are you meeting this? A bus is rushing
by, you don't throw yourself in front of it; your intelligence says
don't do it. This is not fear—unless you are neurotic or have taken
drugs. Your intelligence, not fear, prevents you.

*Q:* Sir, when you meet a wild animal don't you have to have both
intelligence and a conditioned response?

*K:* No, sir. See it. The moment it is a conditioned response there
is fear involved in it and that is transmitted to the animal, but not
if it is intelligence. So find out for yourself which is operating. If it
is fear, then its action is incomplete and therefore there is a danger from the animal; but in the action of intelligence there is no
fear at all.

*Q:* You are saying that if I watch the bear with this intelligence, I
can be killed by the bear without experiencing fear.

*Q2:* If I hadn't met a bear before, I wouldn't even know it was a
bear.

*K:* You are all making such complications. This is so simple. Now
leave the animals alone. Let us start with ourselves; we are partly
animals too.

　　　The effects of fear and its actions based on past memories are destructive, contradictory, and paralysing. Do we see that?
Not verbally but actually; that when you are afraid you are com-

pletely isolated and any action that takes place from that isolation must be fragmentary and therefore contradictory; therefore, there is struggle, pain, and all the rest of it. Now, an action of awareness of fear without all the responses of memory is a complete action. Try it! Do it! Become aware as you are walking alone when you go home; your old fears will come up. Then watch, be aware whether those fears are actual fears, or projected by thought as memory. As the fear arises, see whether you are watching from the response of thought, or whether you are merely watching. What we are talking about is action, because life is action. We are not saying only one part of life is action. The whole of living is action and that action is broken up; the breaking up of action is this process of memory, with its thoughts and isolation. Is that clear?

*Q:* You mean the idea is to experience totally every split second, without memory entering?

*K:* Sir, when you put a question like that, you have to investigate the question of memory. You have to have memory—the clearer, the more definite, the better. If you are to function technologically, or even if you want to get home, you have to have memory. But thought as the response of memory, and projecting fear out of that memory, is an action that is entirely different.

Now, what is fear? How does it happen that there is fear? How do these fears take place? Would you tell me please?

*Q:* In me it is the attachment to the past.

*K:* Let's take that one thing. What do you mean by that word *attachment?*

*Q:* The mind is holding on to something.

*K:* That is, the mind is holding on to some memory. 'When I was young, how lovely everything was'. Or, I am holding on to something that might happen; so I have cultivated a belief that will protect me. I am attached to a memory, I am attached to a piece of furniture, I am attached to what I am writing because through writing I will become famous. I am attached to a name, to a family, to a house, to various memories, and so on. I have identified myself with all that. Why does this attachment take place?

*Q:* Isn't it because fear is the very basis of our civilization?

*K:* No, sir; why are you attached? What does that word *attachment* signify? I depend upon something. I depend on you all attending, so that I can talk to you; I am depending on you and therefore I am attached to you, because through that attachment I gain a certain energy, a certain élan, and all the rest of that rubbish! So I am attached, which means what? I depend on you; I depend on the furniture. In being attached to the furniture, to a belief, to a book, to the family, to a wife, I am dependent on that to give me comfort, prestige, social position. So dependence is a form of attachment. Now why do I depend? Don't answer me, look at it in yourself. You depend on something, don't you? On your country, on your gods, on your beliefs, on the drugs you take, on drink!

*Q:* It is part of social conditioning.

*K:* Is it social conditioning that makes you depend? Which means you are part of society; society is not independent of you. You have made society, which is corrupt; you have put it together. In that cage you are caught, you are part of it. So don't blame society. Do you see the implications of dependency? What is involved? Why are you depending?

*Q:* So as not to feel lonely.

*K:* Wait, listen quietly. I depend on something because that something fills my emptiness. I depend on knowledge, on books, because that covers my emptiness, my shallowness, my stupidity; so knowledge becomes extraordinarily important. I talk about the beauty of pictures because in myself I depend on that. So dependence indicates my emptiness, my loneliness, my insufficiency, and that makes me depend on you. That is a fact isn't it? Don't theorize, don't argue with it, it is so. If I were not empty, if I were not insufficient, I wouldn't care what you said or did. I wouldn't depend on anything. Because I am empty and lonely I don't know what to do with my life. I write a stupid book and that fills my vanity. So I depend, which means I am afraid of being lonely; I am afraid of my emptiness. Therefore, I fill it with material things or with ideas, or with people.

Aren't you afraid of uncovering your loneliness? Have you uncovered your loneliness, your insufficiency, your emptiness? That is taking place now, isn't it? Therefore, you are afraid of that emptiness now. What are you going to do? What is taking place? Before, you were attached to people, to ideas, to all kinds of things and you see that dependence covers your emptiness, your shallowness. When you see that, you are free aren't you? Now what is the response? Is that fear the response of memory? Or is that fear actual; do you see it?

I work hard for you, don't I? (Laughter) There was a cartoon yesterday morning: A little boy says to another boy, 'When I grow up I am going to be a great prophet; I am going to speak of profound truths, but nobody will listen'. And the other little boy says, 'Then why will you talk, if nobody is going to listen?' 'Ah', he said, 'we prophets are very obstinate'. (Laughter)

So now you have uncovered your fear through attachment, which is dependency. When you look into it you see your emptiness, your shallowness, your pettiness and you are frightened by it. What takes place then? See it, sirs?

*Q:* I try to escape.

*K:* You try to escape through attachment, through dependency. Therefore, you are back again in the old pattern. But if you see the truth that attachment and dependency cover your emptiness, you won't escape, will you? If you don't see the fact of that, you are bound to run away. You will try to fill that emptiness in other ways. Before, you filled it with drugs, now you fill it with sex or with something else. So when you see the fact of that, what has happened? Proceed, sirs, go on with it! I have been attached to the house, to my wife, to books, to my writing, to becoming famous; I see fear arises because I don't know what to do with my emptiness and therefore I depend, therefore I am attached. What do I do when I get this feeling of great emptiness in me?

*Q:* There is a strong feeling.

*K:* Which is fear. I discover I am frightened; therefore, I am attached. Is that fear the response of memory, or is that fear an actual discovery? Discovery is something entirely different from the response of the past. Now which is it with you? Is it the actual discovery? Or the response of the past? Don't answer me. Find out, dig into yourself.

# *From* The Impossible Question
## Saanen, 2 August 1970

*Krishnamurti:* I realize I am frightened—why? Is it because I see that I am dead? I am living in the past and I don't know what it means to observe and live in the present; therefore, this is something totally new and I am frightened to do anything new. Which means what? That my brain and my mind have followed the old pattern, the old method; the old way of thinking, living, and working. But to learn, the mind must be free from the past—we have established that as the truth. Now, look what has happened. I have established the fact as truth that there is no learning if the past interferes. And also I realize that I am frightened. So there is a contradiction between the realization that to learn, the mind must be free of the past, and that at the same time I am frightened to do so. In this there is duality. I see, and I am afraid to see.

*Questioner:* Are we always afraid to see new things?

*K:* Aren't we? Aren't we afraid of change?

*Q:* The new is the unknown. We are afraid of the unknown.

*K:* So we cling to the old and this will inevitably breed fear because life is changing; there are social upheavals, there is rioting, there are wars. So there is fear. Now how am I to learn about fear? We have moved away from the previous movement; now we want to learn about the movement of fear. What is the movement of fear? Are you aware that you are afraid? Are you aware that you have fears?

*Q:* Not always.

*K:* Sir, do you know now, are you aware of your fears now? You can resuscitate them, bring them out and say, 'I am afraid of what people might say about me'. So are you aware that you are frightened about death, about losing money, about losing your wife? Are you aware of those fears? Also of physical fears—that you might have pain tomorrow, and so on? If you are aware, what is the movement in it? What takes place when you are aware that you are afraid?

*Q:* I try to get rid of it.

*K:* When you try to get rid of it, what takes place?

*Q:* You repress it.

*K:* Either you repress it or escape from it; there is a conflict between fear and wanting to get rid of it, isn't there? So there is either repression or escape; and in trying to get rid of it there is conflict, which only increases fear.

*Q:* May I ask a question? Isn't the 'me' the brain itself? The brain gets tired of always seeking new experiences and wants relaxation.

*K:* Are you saying that the brain itself is frightened to let go and is the cause of fear? Look, sir, I want to learn about fear; that means I must be curious, I must be passionate. First of all, I must be curious and I cannot be curious if I form a conclusion. So to learn about fear I mustn't be distracted by running away from it; there mustn't be a movement of repression, which again means a distraction from fear. There mustn't be the feeling 'I must get rid of it'. If I have these feelings I cannot learn. Now, have I these feelings when I see there is fear? I am not saying you shouldn't have these feelings—they are there. If I am aware of them what shall I do? My fears are so strong that I want to run away from them. And the very movement away from them breeds more fear—are you following all this? Do I see the truth and the fact that moving away from fear increases fear? Therefore, there is no movement away from it, right?

*Q:* I don't understand this, because I feel that if I have a fear and I move away from it, I am moving towards something that is going to end that fear, towards something that will see me through it.

*K:* What are you afraid of?

*Q:* Money.

*K:* You are afraid of losing money, not of money. The more the merrier! But you are afraid of losing it, right? Therefore, what do you do? You make quite sure that your money is well placed, but the fear continues. It may not be safe in this changing world, the bank may go bankrupt, and so on. Even though you have plenty of money there is always this fear. Running away from that fear doesn't solve it', nor does suppressing it, saying, 'I won't think about it; for the next second you are thinking about it. So running away from it, avoiding it, doing anything about it, continues fear. That is a fact. Now we have established two facts: that to learn there must be curiosity and there must be no pressure of the past. And to learn about fear there must be no running away from fear. That is a fact; that is the truth. Therefore, you don't run away. Now when I don't run away from it what takes place?

*Q:* I stop being identified with it.

*K:* Is that what learning is? You have stopped.

*Q:* I don't know what you mean.

*K:* Stopping is not learning. Because of the desire not to have fear, you want to escape from it. Just see the subtlety of it. I am afraid, and I want to learn about it. I don't know what is going to happen, I want to learn the movement of fear. So what takes place? I am not running away, I am not suppressing, I am not avoiding it: I want to learn about it.

*Q:* I think about how to get rid of it.

*K:* If you want to get rid of it as I have just explained, who is the person who is going to get rid of it? You want to get rid of it, which means you resist it, therefore fear increases. If you don't see the fact of that, I am sorry, I can't help you.

*Q:* We must accept fear.

*K:* I don't accept fear. Who is the entity who is accepting fear?

*Q:* If one cannot escape, one must accept.

*K:* To escape from it, to avoid it, to pick up a novel and read what other people are doing, to look at television, to go to the temple or to church—all that is still avoidance of fear, and any avoidance of it only increases and strengthens fear. That is a fact. After establishing that fact I won't run away, I won't suppress. I am learning not running away. Therefore, what takes place when there's an awareness of fear?

*Q:* Understanding of the process of fear.

*K:* We are doing it. I am understanding the process, I am watching it, I am learning about it. I am afraid and I am not running away from it; now what takes place?

*Q:* You are face-to-face with fear.

*K:* What takes place then?

*Q:* There is no movement in any direction.

*K:* Don't you ask this question? Please, just listen to me. I am not running away, I am not suppressing, I am not avoiding, I am not resisting it. There it is, I am watching it. The natural question arising out of that is: Who is watching this fear? Please don't guess. When you say, 'I am watching fear, I am learning about fear', who is the entity that is watching it?

*Q:* Fear itself.

*K:* Is fear itself watching itself? Please don't guess. Don't come to any conclusion, find out. The mind isn't escaping from fear, not building a wall against fear through courage and all the rest of it. What takes place when I watch? I ask myself naturally: Who is watching the thing called fear? Don't answer me, please. I have raised the question, not you. Sir, find out who is watching this fear: another fragment of me?

*Q:* The entity who is watching cannot be the result of the past, it must be fresh, something that happens at this moment.

*K:* I am not talking about whether the watching is the result of the past. I am watching, I am aware of fear, I am aware that I am frightened of losing money, of becoming ill, of my wife leaving me and God knows what else. And I want to learn about it; therefore, I am watching and my natural question is: Who is watching this fear?

*Q:* My image of myself.

*K:* When I ask the question: 'Who is watching', what takes place? In the very question there is a division, isn't there? That is a fact. When I say, 'Who is watching,' it means the thing is there and I am watching, therefore there is a division. Now why is there a division? You answer me this, don't guess, don't repeat what somebody else has said, including myself. Find out why this division exists at the moment when you ask the question: 'Who is watching?' Find out.

*Q:* There is a desire on my part to watch.

*K:* Which means the desire says, 'Watch in order to escape'—you follow? You said before, 'I have understood that I mustn't escape', and now you find that desire is making you escape subtly; therefore, you are still watching fear as an outsider. See the importance of this. You are watching with an intention to get rid of fear. And we said a few minutes ago, to try to get rid of fear means first censoring fear. So your watching implies trying to get rid of fear; therefore, there is a division that only strengthens fear. So I am again asking the question: Who is watching fear?

*Q:* Isn't there also another point: Who is asking the question 'who is watching fear'?

*K:* I am asking that question, sir.

*Q:* But who is asking the question?

*K:* The same thing, only you push it further back. Now, please listen: this is the most practical way of going about it. You will see if you follow this very carefully that the mind will be free of fear, but you are not doing it.

    I am frightened of losing money and therefore what do I do? I escape by avoiding thinking about it. So I realize how silly it is to avoid it, because the more I resist it the more I am afraid. I am watching it and the question arises: Who is watching it? Is it the desire that wants to get rid of it, go beyond it, be free of it, that is watching? It is. And I know that watching it that way only divides and therefore strengthens fear. So I see the truth of that; therefore, desire to get rid of it has gone—you follow me? It's like seeing a poisonous snake: the desire to touch it is finished with. The desire to take drugs is finished when I see the real danger of them; I won't touch them. As long as I don't see the danger of it, I'll go on. In the same way, as long as I don't see that running away from fear strengthens fear, I'll go on running away. The moment I see it I won't run. Then what happens?

*Q:* How can a person who is afraid of being involved look? One is scared.

*K:* I am pointing it out to you. The moment you are scared of looking at fear, you won't learn about it, and if you want to learn about fear, don't be scared. It is as simple as that. If I don't know how to swim I won't plunge into the river. When I know that fear cannot possibly be ended if I am afraid to look and if I really want to look, I'll say, 'I don't care, I'll look'.

*Q:* It was said, it is desire to get away from fear that constantly breeds more fear. When I'm afraid I want to get away from it, so what I always do is to let it be relative so that I can identify with it, so that I can unify myself.

K: You see that! It is all these tricks that we are playing on ourselves. Do listen, sir. Who is saying all this? You make an effort to identify yourself with fear.

*Q:* I am that fear.

*K:* Ah! Wait. If you are that fear, as you say you are, then what happens?

*Q:* When I come to terms with it, it begins to diminish.

*K:* No. Not coming to terms! When you say that you are fear, fear is not something separate from you. What takes place? I am brown. I am afraid to be brown, but I say, 'Yes, I am brown' and that's the end of it, isn't it? I am not running away from it. What takes place then?

*Q:* Acceptance.

*K:* Do I accept it? On the contrary, I forget that I am brown. I want to learn about myself. I must know myself completely, passionately, because that is the foundation of all action; without that I'll lead a life of utter confusion. To learn about myself I cannot follow anybody. If I follow anybody I am not learning. Learning implies that the past does not interfere, because myself is something extraordinary, vital, moving, dynamic; so I must look at it afresh with a new mind. There is no new mind if the past is always operating. That is a fact, I see that. Then in seeing that I realize I am frightened. I don't know what will happen. So I want to learn about fear—you follow? I am moving all the time in the movement of learning. I want to know about myself and I realize something—a profound truth. I am going to learn about fear, which means I mustn't run away from it at any price. I mustn't have a subtle form of desire to run away from it. So what happens to a mind that is capable of looking at fear without division? The division being trying to get rid of it, subtle forms of escape, suppression, and so on. What happens to the mind when it is confronted with fear and there is no question of running away from it? Please, find out, give your mind to it.

# Saanen, 25 July 1972

SORROW EXISTS WHEN there is fear. So one must go into the question of fear. What does a particular human being fear? What does fear mean basically? The sense of insecurity? A child demands complete security; and more and more the mother and the father are working, homes are broken up, the parents are so deeply concerned about themselves, their position in society, having more money, more refrigerators, more cars, more this and more that, they have no time to give complete security to the child. Security is one of the essential things of life, not only for you and me, but for everybody. For those who live in ghettos or those who live in palaces, security is absolutely necessary. Otherwise the brain can't function efficiently, sanely. Watch this process. I need security, I must have food, clothes, and shelter; so must everybody. And if I am lucky I can arrange it physically. But psychologically it is much more difficult to become completely secure. So I seek that security in a belief, in a conclusion, in nationality, in a family, or in my experience, and when that experience, that family, that belief is threatened, there is fear. There is fear when I have to face psychological danger, which is uncertainty, meeting something I don't know, the tomorrow. Then there is fear. And there is fear also when I am comparing myself with you whom I think are greater.

# Saanen, 2 August 1962

I WOULD LIKE to talk about something with which some of you are perhaps not very familiar, and that is the question of emptying the mind of fear. I would like to go into it rather deeply, but not in great detail, because one can supply the details for oneself.

Is it possible for the mind to empty itself totally of fear? Fear of any kind breeds illusion; it makes the mind dull, shallow. Where there is fear there is obviously no freedom, and without freedom there is no love at all. And most of us have some form of fear: fear of darkness, fear of public opinion, fear of snakes, fear of physical pain, fear of old age, fear of death. We have literally dozens of fears. And is it possible to be completely free of fear?

We can see what fear does to each one of us. It makes one tell lies, it corrupts one in various ways, it makes the mind empty, shallow. There are dark corners in the mind that can never be investigated and exposed as long as one is afraid. Physical self-protection, the instinctive urge to keep away from the venomous snake, to draw back from the precipice, to avoid falling under the tramcar, and so on, is sane, normal, healthy. But I am talking about the psychological self-protectiveness that makes one afraid of disease, of death, of an enemy. When we seek fulfilment in any form, whether through painting, through music, through relationship, or what you will, there is always fear. So, what is important is to be aware of this whole process in oneself, to observe, to learn about it, and not ask how to get rid of fear. When you merely want to get rid of fear you will find ways and means of escaping from it, and so there can never be freedom from fear.

If you consider what fear is and how to approach it, you will see that for most of us the word is much more important than the fact. Take the word *loneliness*. By that word I mean the sense of isolation that suddenly comes upon one for no apparent reason. I don't know if this has ever happened to you. Though you may be surrounded by your family, by your neighbours, though you may be walking with friends or riding in a crowded bus, suddenly you feel completely isolated. From the memory of that experience there is fear of isolation, of being lonely. Or you are attached to someone who dies, and you find yourself left alone, isolated. Feeling that sense of isolation, you escape from it by means of the radio, the cinema, or you turn to sex, to drink, or you go to church, worship God. Whether you go to church or take a pill it is an escape, and all escapes are essentially the same.

Now, the word *loneliness* prevents us from entering into a complete understanding of that state. The word, associated with past experience, evokes the feeling of danger and creates fear; therefore, we try to run away. Please watch yourself as in a mirror, do not just listen to me, and you will see that the word has extraordinary significance for most of us. Words like *God, communism, hell, heaven, loneliness, wife, family*—what an astonishing influence they have on us. We are slaves to such words, and the mind that is a slave to words is never free of fear.

To be aware of and learn about fear in oneself is not to interpret that feeling in words, for words are associated with the past, with knowledge; and in the very movement of learning about fear without verbalization, which is not to acquire knowledge about it, you will find there is a total emptying of the mind of all fear. This means that one has to go very deeply into oneself, putting aside all words; and when the mind understands the whole content of fear and is therefore empty of fear, both conscious and unconscious, then there comes a state of innocency.

For most Christians, that word *innocency* is merely a symbol; but I am talking of actually being in a state of innocency, which means having no fear, and therefore the mind is completely mature, instantly, without going through the passage of time. And that is possible only when there is total attention, an awareness of every thought, of every word, of every gesture. The mind is attentive without the barrier of words, without interpretation, justification, or condemnation. Such a mind is a light unto itself; and a mind that is a light unto itself has no fear.

# Rome, 7 April 1966

IF YOU ARE living in a small village, then it does count a great deal what your neighbour thinks of you. There is the fear of not being able to fulfil, not being able to achieve what you want, not being successful. You know the various types of fear.

Mere resistance to fear is not an end to fear. Verbally, intellectually, you may be clever enough to rationalize fear and build a wall against it, yet behind that wall there is this constant gnawing of fear. Unless you are free from fear, you can't think, feel, or live properly. You are living in darkness. Religions have cultivated that fear through hell and all that business. There is the fear of the State and its tyranny. You must think of the public, the state, the dictators, the people who know what is good for you, the Big Brother and the Big Father. Is it possible actually to be totally free of fear? If you can discuss it, you can learn about it. If you say, 'I can't get rid of it; what am I to do?', there is no problem. Someone will tell you what to do, but you will always be dependent on that person, and you will enter another field of fear.

*Questioner:* The awareness of our danger and therefore fear might present a certain problem.

*Krishnamurti:* No, it is a healthy response; otherwise you'd be killed. When you come to a precipice, and you just are not afraid or don't pay attention, you are in great danger, but that fear, the bodily fear, creates a psychological fear too. It is a very complex problem; it isn't just a matter of saying, 'I have fear about something or other, and let me wipe it out'. In order to understand it you must first be very clear about words; you must realize that the word is not the fact of fear, but the word engenders fear; unconsciously the whole structure is verbal. The word *culture* brings a deep response from memory—Italian culture, European culture, Hindu culture, Japanese culture, Chinese culture. It is very interesting to go into it. The unconscious is made up of memories, of experiences, traditions, propaganda, words. You have an experience, and you react. That reaction is translated into words: 'I was happy', 'I was unhappy', 'He hurt me', and those words remain. They awaken and strengthen the daily experience.

Say you have insulted me; it has left a mark, and that mark is strengthened, deepened by the word, by the memory associated with that feeling, which is really a word, a tradition. It is important to understand this. In certain countries in Asia, in India, among certain groups of people, tradition is immense, much stronger than here, because they have lived longer; they are an old country, much more deep-rooted, with a tradition of ten thousand years and more. The word brings up memories and associations, which are all part of the unconscious, and it also brings about fear.

Take the word *cancer*. You hear the word and immediately all the ideas and the thoughts about cancer come rushing in—the pain, the agony, the suffering, and the question, 'Do I have cancer?'. The word is extraordinarily important to us. The word, the sentence, when organized becomes an idea—based on a formula, and that holds us.

The word is not the fact; the word *microphone* is not the microphone. But a word brings fear or pleasure into being through association and remembrance. We are slaves to words and to examine anything fully, to look, we must be free of the word. If I'm a Hindu and a Brahmin, a Catholic, a Protestant, an Anglican, or a Presbyterian, to look I have to be free of that word, with all its associations, and that's extraordinarily difficult. The difficulty disappears when we are passionately inquiring, examining.

The unconscious is stored-up memory; the unconscious, through a word, becomes alive. Through a smell, or through seeing a flower, you associate immediately. The storehouse, the stored-up, is the unconscious, and we make a tremendous lot of ado about it. It is really nothing at all. It is as trivial and superficial as the conscious mind. Both can be healthy, and both can be unhealthy.

The word brings on fear, and the word is not the fact. What is fear? What am I afraid of? Please, we're discussing. Take your own fear. It may be fear of your wife, of losing your job or your fame.

What is fear? Let us take a problem like death for the moment. It is a very complex problem. I am afraid of death. How does this fear arise? Obviously it arises through thought. I have seen people die. I also may die, painfully or quietly, and thinking has brought on this fear.

*Q:* One of the strongest fears is the fear of the unknown.

*K:* It is the unknown. I'm taking that as an example. Substitute your own fear—fear of your husband, of your wife, of your neighbour, of ill health, of not being able to fulfil, of not loving, of not having enough love, of not having intelligence.

*Q:* Surely in some cases it's justified. Take, for instance, if a man is afraid of his wife.

*K:* All right; he is married and is afraid of his wife.

*Q:* Or he's afraid of his boss, or afraid he may lose his job.

*K:* Wait. Why should he be afraid? We are discussing fear, not of the job, of the boss, of the wife. Fear exists always in relation to something; it doesn't exist abstractly. I'm afraid of my boss, my wife, my neighbour, of death. It is in relation to something. I took death as an example. I'm afraid of it. Why? What brings on this fear? Obviously it is thought. Visually I have seen death, people dying. Associated with that, identified with that, is the fact that I, myself, will die one of these days. Thought thinks about it; there is a thinking about it. Death is something unavoidable, and something to be pushed as far away as possible. I can't push it far away except with thought. I have a distance, so many years allotted to me. When it comes time for me to go, I'll go; but in the meantime I've kept it away. Thought, through association, through identification, through memory, through the religious or social environment, through economic conditioning, rationalizes it, accepts it, or invents a hereafter. Can I come into contact with a fact? I'm afraid of my wife. That will be much simpler. She dominates me. I can give a dozen reasons for my fear of her. I see how fear arises. How am I to be free of it? I can ask her, I can walk out, but that doesn't solve the problem. How am I to be free of that fear? Look at it; I am afraid of my wife. She has an image about me and I have an image about her. There is no actual relationship, except perhaps physically. Otherwise it is purely a relationship between the images. I'm not being cynical, but this is a fact, isn't it? Perhaps those of you who are married know better than I do.

*Q:* Will she have a picture of you being weak, and will you have a picture of her being tough?

*K:* Tough and strong. You have dozens of reasons, sir, but there is no actual relationship at all. To be related means to be in contact. How can one image be related to another image? An image is an idea, a memory, a recollection, a remembrance. If I really want to be free of fear, I have to destroy my image about her, and she has to destroy her image about me. I may destroy mine, or she may destroy hers, but one-sided action doesn't bring about freedom from the relationship that awakens fear. I break my image about you, totally. I look at it, and then I understand what relationship is. I break the image completely. Then I am directly in contact with you, not with your image. But you may not have broken your image, because it gives you pleasure.

*Q:* That's the rub, I haven't broken my image.

*K:* So you keep on, and I say, 'All right; I have no image of you'. I'm not afraid of you. Fear ceases only when there is direct contact. If I have no escapes at any level, I can look at the fact. I can look at the fact that I am going to die, in ten years or in twenty years. I have to understand death, come into contact with it physically, organically, because I'm still alive. I have plenty of energy; I'm still active, healthy. Bodily, I can't die; but psychologically, I can die.

This requires tremendous observation, going into, working. To die means that you have to die every day, not just twenty years from now. You die every day to everything that you know, except technologically. You die to the image of your wife; you die every day to the pleasures you have, to the pains, the memories, the experiences. Otherwise you can't come into contact with them. If you do die to them all, fear comes to an end and there is a renewal.

# *Talk to Students at Rajghat School, 5 January 1954*

I WOULD LIKE to talk of a topic that may be rather difficult, but we will try and make it as simple and direct as possible. You know most of us have some kind of fear, have we not? Do you know your particular fear? You might be afraid of your teacher, of your guardian, of your parents, of the older people, or of a snake, or a buffalo, or of what somebody says, or of death, and so on. Each one has fear; but, for young people, the fears are fairly superficial. As we grow older, the fears become more complex, more difficult, more subtle. You know the words *subtle, complex,* and *difficult,* don't you? For example, I want to fulfil; I am not an old person, and I want to fulfil myself in a particular direction. You know what *fulfilment* means? Every word is difficult, is it not? I want to become a great writer. I feel if I could write, my life would be happy. So I want to write. But something happens to me; I get paralysed and for the rest of my life I am frightened, I am frustrated, I feel I have not lived. So that becomes my fear. So, as we grow older, various forms of fear come into being, fears of being left alone, not having a friend, being lonely, losing property, having no position, and other various types of fear. But we won't go now into the very difficult and subtle types of fear because they require much more thought.

It is very important that we—you young people and I—should consider this question of fear, because society and the older people think fear is necessary to keep you in right behaviour. If you are afraid of your teacher or of your parents, they can control you better, can they not? They can say 'Do this and do not do that' and you will jolly well have to obey them. So, fear is used as a moral pressure. The teachers use fear, say, in a large class, as a means of controlling the students. Is it not so? Society says fear is necessary and that otherwise, the citizens, the people, will just outflow and do things wildly. Fear has thus become a necessity for the control of man.

You know fear is also used to civilize man. Religions throughout the world have used fear as a means of controlling man. Have they not? They say that if you do not do certain things in this life, you will pay for it in the next life. Though all religions preach love, though they preach brotherhood, though they talk about the unity of man, they all subtly, or very brutally, grossly, maintain this sense of fear.

If you have a large number of students in one class, how can the teacher control you? He cannot. He has to invent ways and means of controlling you. So, he says 'Compete. Become like that boy who is much cleverer than you'. So you struggle, you are afraid. Your fear is generally used as a means of controlling you. Do you understand? Is it not very important that education should eradicate fear, should help the students to get rid of fear, because fear corrupts the mind? I think it is very important in a school of this kind that every form of fear should be understood and dispelled, got rid of. Otherwise, if you have any kind of fear, it twists your mind, and you can never be intelligent. Fear is like a dark cloud and, when you have fear, it is like walking in sunshine with a dark cloud in your mind, always frightened.

So, is it not the function of education to be truly educated—that is, to understand fear and to be free of it? For instance, suppose you go off without telling your housemaster or teacher and you come back and invent stories saying that you have been with some people, while you have been to a cinema, which means you are frightened. If you are not frightened of the teacher, you think you would do what you like and the teachers think the same. But to understand fear implies a great deal, much more than doing exactly what you want to do. You know there are natural reactions of the body, are there not? When you see a snake, you jump. That is not fear, because that is the natural reaction of the body. In front of danger, the body reacts; it jumps. When you see a precipice, you do not walk just blindly along. That is not fear. When you see a danger, or a car coming very fast, you sweep out of the way. It is not an indication of fear. Those are bodily responses to protect itself against danger; such reactions are not fear.

Fear comes in, does it not, when you want to do something and you are prevented from doing it? That is one type of fear. You want to go to a cinema; you would like to go out to Benares for the day and the teacher says no. There are regulations and you do not like these regulations. You like to go. So you go on some excuse and you come back. The teacher finds out that you have gone, and you are afraid of punishment. So, fear comes in, when there is a feeling that you are going to be punished. But if the teacher talks over smoothly why you should not go to town, explains to you the dangers, eating of food which is not clean and so on, you understand. Even if he has not the time to explain to you and go into the whole problem of why you should not go, because you also think, your intelligence is awakened to find out why you should not go. Then, there is no problem, you do not go. If you want to go, you talk it over and find out.

To do just what you like in order to show that you are free from fear is not intelligence. Courage is not the opposite of fear. You know in the battlefields they are very courageous. For various reasons they take drinks, or do all kinds of things to feel courageous; but that is not freedom from fear. We won't go into it, let us leave it at that.

Should not education help the students to be free from fear of every kind—which means, from now on to understand all the problems of life, problems of sex, problems of death, of public opinion, of authority? I am going to discuss all these things, so that when you leave this place, though there are fears in the world, though you have your own ambitions, your own desires, you will understand and so be free from fear, because you know fear is very dangerous. All people are afraid of something or other. Most people do not want to make a mistake, do not want to go wrong, specially when they are young. So they think that if they could follow somebody, if they could listen to somebody, they will be told what to do and, by doing that, they will achieve an end, a purpose.

Most of us are very conservative. You know what that word means, you know what it is to conserve? To hold, to guard. Most of us want to remain respectable and so we want to do the right thing, we want to follow the right conduct, which, if you go into it very deeply, you will see is an indication of fear. Why not make a mistake, why not find out? But the man who is afraid is always thinking 'I must do the right thing, I must look respectable, I must not let the public think what I am or not'. Such a man is really, fundamentally, basically, afraid. A man who is ambitious is really a frightened person, and a man who is frightened has no love, has no sympathy. It is like a person enclosed behind a wall, in a house. It is very important—while we are young—to understand this thing, to understand fear. It is fear that makes us obey, but if we can talk it over, reason together, discuss and think together, then I may understand it and do it; but to compel me, to force me, to do a thing that I do not understand because I am frightened of you, is wrong education. Is it not?

So, I feel it is very important in a place like this that both the educator and the educated should understand this problem. Creativity, to be creative—you know what it means? To write a poem is partly creative, to paint a picture, to look at a tree, to love the tree, the river, the birds, the people, the earth, the feeling that the earth is ours—that is partly creative. But that feeling is destroyed when you have fear, when you say 'this is mine, my country, my class, my group, my philosophy, my religion'. When you have that kind of feeling, you are not creative, because it is the instinct of fear that is dictating this feeling of 'mine', 'my country'. After all, the earth is not yours or mine; it is ours. And if we can think in those terms, we will create quite a different world—not an American world or a Russian world or an Indian world, but it will be our world, yours and mine, the rich man's and the poor man's. But the difficulty is: when there is fear, we do not create. A person who is afraid can never find truth or God. Behind all our worships, all our images, all our rituals, there is fear and, therefore, your gods are not gods, they are stones.

So, it is very important, while we are young, to understand this thing; and you can only understand it when you know that you are afraid, when you can look at your own fears. But that requires a great deal of insight, which we want to discuss now. Because it is a much deeper problem, which the older people can discuss, we will discuss that with the teachers. But it is the function of the educator to help the educated to understand fear. It is for the teachers to help you to understand your fear and not to suppress it, not to hold you down, so that when you leave this place, your mind is very clear, sharp, unspoiled by fear. As I was saying yesterday, the old people have not created a beautiful world, they are full of darkness, fear, corruption, competition; they have not created a good world. Perhaps if you, going out of this place, out of Rajghat, can really be free from fear of every kind or understand how to meet fear in yourself and in others, then perhaps you will create quite a different world, not a world of the Communist or of the congressite, and so on, but a totally different world. Truly, that is the function of education.

*Student:* How do we get rid of fear?

*Krishnamurti:* You want to know how to get rid of fear? Do you know what you are afraid of? Go slowly with me. Fear is something in relation to something else. Fear does not exist by itself. It exists in relation to a snake, to what my parents might say to a teacher, to death; it is in connection with something. Do you understand? Fear is not a thing by itself, it exists in contact, in relation, in touch with something else. Are you conscious, aware that you are afraid in relation to something else? Do you know you are afraid? Are you not afraid of your parents, are you not afraid of your teachers? I hope not, but probably you are. Are you not afraid that you might not pass your examinations? Are you not afraid that people should think of you nicely and decently and say what a great man you are? Are you not afraid; don't you know your fears? I am trying to show how you have fear, you and I have lost interest already. So first you must know what you are afraid of. I will explain to you very slowly. Then you must also know the mind, must know why it is afraid. Is fear something apart from the mind, and does not the mind create fear, either because it has remembered or it projects itself into the future? You had better pester your teachers till they explain to you all these things. You spend an hour every day over mathematics or geography, but you do not spend even two minutes about the most important problem of life. Should you not spend with your teachers much more time over this, how to be free from fear, rather than merely discussing mathematics or reading a textbook?

A school based on fear of any kind is a rotten school, it should not be. It requires a great deal of intelligence on the part of the teachers and the boys to understand this problem. Fear corrupts, and to be free from fear one has to understand how the mind creates fear. There is no such thing as fear but what the mind creates. The mind wants shelter, the mind wants security, the mind has various forms of self-protective ambition; and as long as all that exists, you will have fear. It is very important to understand ambition, to understand authority; both are indications of this term, which is destruction.

# *Paris, 22 May 1966*

MOST PEOPLE ARE afraid, both physically and inwardly. Fear exists only in relationship to something. I am afraid of illness, of physical pain. I've had it and I'm afraid of it. I'm afraid of public opinion. I'm afraid of losing a job. I'm afraid of not arriving, achieving, not being able to fulfil. I'm afraid of darkness, afraid of my own stupidity, afraid of my own pettiness. We have so many different fears, and we try to solve these fears in fragments. We don't seem to be able to go beyond that. If we think we have understood one particular fear, and have resolved it, another fear comes up. When we are aware that we are afraid, we try to run away from it, try to find an answer, try to find out what to do, or try to suppress it.

We human beings have cunningly developed a network of escapes: God, amusement, drink, sex, anything. All escapes are the same, whether it is in the name of God or drink! If we are to live as human beings we have to solve the problem. If we live in fear, conscious or unconscious, it's like living in darkness, with tremendous inward conflict and resistance. The greater the fear, the greater the tension, the greater the neuroticism, the greater is the urge to escape. If we do not escape, then we ask ourselves, 'How are we to solve it?' We seek ways and means of solving it, but always within the field of the known. We do something about it, and this action bred by thought is action within the field of experience, knowledge, the known, and therefore, there is no answer. That's what we do, and we die with fear. We live throughout our lives with fear and die with fear. Now can a human being totally eradicate fear? Can we do anything, or nothing? The nothing does not mean that we accept fear, rationalize it, and live with it; that's not the inaction of which we are talking.

We have done everything we can with regard to fear. We have analysed it, gone into it, tried to face it, come into direct contact with it, resisted it, done everything possible, and the thing remains. Is it possible to be aware of it totally, not merely intellectually, emotionally, but be completely aware of it, and yet not *do* something about it? We must come into contact with fear, but we don't. The word *fear* has caused that fear. The word itself keeps us from being in contact with the fact.

# *From* Beyond Violence
## *San Diego State College, 6 April 1970*

WE SHOULD GO into the question of fear completely, understand it fully, so that we shall be rid of it. It can be done; it is not just a theory, or a hope. If one gives complete attention to this question of fear, to how one approaches it, looks at it, then one will find that the mind—the mind that has suffered so much, that has endured so much pain, that has lived with great sorrow and fear—will be completely free of it. To go into this it is absolutely essential that one has no prejudice that will prevent one from understanding the truth of 'what is'. To take this journey together implies neither acceptance nor denial; neither saying to oneself that it is absolutely impossible to be rid of fear, nor that it is possible. One needs a free mind to inquire into this question; a mind that, having reached no conclusion, is free to observe, to inquire.

There are so many forms of psychological and psychosomatic fear. To go into each one of these various forms of fear, into every aspect, would take an enormous amount of time. But one can observe the general quality of fear; one can observe the general nature and structure of fear without getting lost in the detail of a particular form of one's fears. When one understands the nature and structure of fear as such, then one can approach, with that understanding, the particular fear.

One may be afraid of the dark; one may be afraid of one's wife or husband, or of what the public says or thinks or does; one may be afraid of the sense of loneliness, or of the emptiness of life, the boredom of the meaningless existence that one leads. One may be afraid of the future, of the uncertainty and insecurity of tomorrow—or of the bomb. One may be afraid of death, the ending of one's life. There are so many forms of fear, the neurotic as well as the sane, rational fears—if fear can ever be rational or sane. Most of us are neurotically afraid of the past, of today, and of tomorrow; so that time is involved in fear.

There are not only the conscious fears of which one is aware, but also those that are deep down, undiscovered in the deep recesses of one's mind. How is one to deal with conscious fears as well as those that are hidden? Surely fear is in the movement away from 'what is'; it is the flight, the escape, the avoidance of, actually, that brings about fear. Also, when there is comparison, of any kind, there is the breeding of fear—the comparison of what you are with what you think you should be. So fear is in the movement away from what is actual, not in the object from which you move away.

None of these problems of fear can be resolved through will—saying to oneself, 'I will not be afraid'. Such acts of will have no meaning.

We are considering a very serious problem to which one has to give one's complete attention. One cannot give attention if one is interpreting or translating or comparing what is being said with what one already knows. One has to listen—an art one has to learn, for normally one is always comparing, evaluating, judging, agreeing, denying, and one does not listen at all; actually one prevents oneself from listening. To listen so completely implies that one gives one's whole attention—it does not mean one agrees or disagrees. There is no agreement or disagreement when we are exploring together; but the 'microscope' through which one looks may not be clear. If one looks through a precision instrument, then what one sees is what another will also see; therefore, there is no question of agreement or disagreement. In trying to examine this whole question of fear one has to give one's whole attention; and yet, until fear is resolved it deadens the mind, makes it insensitive, dull.

How does it happen that the hidden fears are exposed? One can know the conscious fears—how to deal with them will come presently—but there are hidden fears, which are perhaps much more important. So how will one deal with them, how will one expose them? Can they be exposed through analysis, seeking their cause? Will analysis free the mind from fear, not a particular neurotic fear, but the whole structure of fear? In analysis is implied not only time but the analyser—taking many, many days, years, even the whole of one's life, at the end of which perhaps you have understood a little, but you are ready for the grave. Who is the analyser? If he is the professional, the expert who has a degree, he will also take time; he also is the result of many forms of conditioning. If one analyses oneself there is implied the analyser, who is the censor, and he is going to analyse the fear that he himself has created. In any event, analysis takes time; in the interval between that which you are analysing and its ending many other factors will arise that give it a different direction. You have to see the truth that analysis is not the way, because the analyser is a fragment among the many other fragments that go to make up the 'me', the I, the ego—he is the result of time, he is conditioned. To see that analysis implies time and does not bring the ending of fear means that you have completely put aside the whole idea of progressive change; you have seen that the very factor of change is one of the major causes of fear.

To the speaker, this is very important; therefore, he feels very strongly, he speaks intensely; but he is not doing propaganda—there is nothing for you to join, nothing for you to believe; but observe and learn and be free of this fear.

So analysis is not the way. When you see the truth of that, it means you are no longer thinking in terms of the analyser who is going to analyse, going to judge and evaluate, and your mind is free of that particular burden called analysis; therefore, it is capable of looking directly.

How are you to look at this fear; how are you to bring out all its structure, all its hidden parts? Through dreams? Dreams are the continuation of the activity of waking hours during sleep—arc they not? You observe in dreams that there is always action, something or other is happening in dreams as in the waking hours, a continuation that is still part of one whole movement. So dreams have no value. You see what is happening: we are eliminating the things to which you are accustomed—analysis, dreams, will, time; when you eliminate all those, the mind becomes extraordinarily sensitive—not only sensitive but intelligent. Now, with that sensitivity and intelligence we are going to look at fear. If you really go into this, you turn your back on the whole of the social structure in which time, analysis, and will are in operation. What is fear? How does it come? Fear is always in relation to something; it does not exist by itself. There is fear of what happened yesterday in relation to the possibility of its repetition tomorrow; there is always a fixed point from which relationship takes place. How does fear come into this? I had pain yesterday; there is the memory of it and I do not want it again tomorrow. Thinking about the pain of yesterday, thinking that involves the memory of yesterday's pain, projects the fear of having pain again tomorrow. So it is thought that brings about fear. Thought breeds fear; thought also cultivates pleasure. To understand fear you must also understand pleasure—they are interrelated; without understanding one you cannot understand the other. This means that one cannot say, 'I must have only pleasure and no fear'; fear is the other side of the coin that is called pleasure.

# Bombay, 22 February 1961

NOW LET US consider the totality of fear. A mind that is afraid, that has deep within itself anxiety, a sense of fear, and the hope that is born out of fear and despair—such a mind obviously is an unhealthy mind. Such a mind may go to temples, churches; it may spin every kind of theory, it may pray, it may be very scholastic, may outwardly have all the polish of sophistication, obey, have good manners and politeness, and behave righteously outwardly; but such a mind that has all these things and its roots in fear—as most of our minds have—obviously cannot see things straight. Fear does breed various forms of mental illnesses. No one is afraid of God; but one is afraid of public opinion, afraid of not achieving, not fulfilling, afraid of not having the opportunity; and through it all there is this extraordinary sense of guilt—one has done a thing that one should not have done; the sense of guilt in the very act of doing; one is healthy and others are poor and unhealthy; one has food and others have no food. The more the mind is inquiring, penetrating, asking, the greater the sense of guilt, anxiety. And if this whole process is not understood, if this whole totality of fear is not understood, it does lead to peculiar activities, the activities of the saints, the activities of politicians—activities that are all ex-plainable, if you watch, if you are aware of this contradictory nature in fear, both the conscious and the unconscious. You know fear—fear of death, fear of not being loved or fear of loving, fear of losing, fear of gain. How do you tackle this?

Fear is the urge that seeks a master, a guru; fear is this coating of respectability, which every one loves so dearly—to be respectable. I am not talking of anything that is not a fact. So you can see it in your everyday life. This extraordinary, pervasive nature of fear—how do you deal with it? Do you merely develop the quality of courage in order to meet the demand of fear? You understand? Do you determine to be courageous to face events in life, or merely rationalize fear away, or find explanations that will give satisfaction to the mind that is caught in fear? How do you deal with it? Turn on the radio, read a book, go to a temple, cling to some form of dogma, belief? Let us discuss how to deal with fear. If you are aware of it, what is the manner of your approach to this shadow? Obviously one can see very clearly that a mind that is afraid withers away; it cannot function properly; it cannot think reasonably. By fear I do not mean the fear at the conscious level only, but also in the deep recesses of one's own mind and heart. How do you discover it, and when you do discover it what do you do? I am not asking a rhetorical question; don't say, 'He will answer it'. I will answer it, but you will have to find out. The moment there is no fear, there is no ambition, but there is an action, which is for the love of the thing but not for recognition of the thing that you are doing. So, how do you deal with it? What is your response?

Obviously, the everyday response to fear is to push it aside and run away from it, to cover it up through will, determination, resistance, escape. That is what we do, sirs. I am not saying anything extraordinary. And so fear goes on pursuing you like a shadow, you are not free of it. I am talking of the totality of fear, not just a particular state of fear—death, or what your neighbour will say; fear of one's husband or son dying; of one's wife running away. You know what fear is? Each one has his own particular form of fear—not one but multiple fears. A mind that has any form of fear cannot, obviously, have the quality of love, sympathy, tenderness. Fear is the destructive energy in man. It withers the mind, it distorts thought, it leads to all kinds of extraordinarily clever and subtle theories, absurd superstitions, dogmas, and beliefs. If you see that fear is destructive, then how do you proceed to wipe the mind clean?

# Bombay, 22 January 1978

WE ARE INVESTIGATING fear. To go into the root of fear we must understand why the brain, thought, lives in images. Why do you create and live with images, pictures, about the future, about your wife, your husband, about the speaker, and so on? Why do you create pictures? If you don't create pictures and images, is there fear? We must first go into the question of why thought breeds these complicated pictures, images, in which we live. We must ask what thought is. We are investigating into fear and to go into that very deeply you must inquire into why thought creates the picture of the future or of the past, which breeds fear, and into what thought is. Unless you understand this you will not come face to face with fear. You will avoid it. You will run away from it. Because fear is a living thing. You can't control it, you can't put a lid on it.

IF YOU ACT through fear you are lost. Fear and love cannot exist together. In this country there is no love. There is devotion, reverence, but no love. Devotion to your guru, to your gods, to your ideals, is self-worship. It is self-worship because you have created your guru, your ideals, your gods; you have created them, thought has created them, your grandfather has, and you accept this because it satisfies you, it gives you comfort. So what you are devoted to is yourself. Swallow that pill and live with it! So we are saying that, as love cannot exist with fear, and we live in fear, the other thing is not. And when you have the other thing you have all life, and then, do what you will, it will be right action. But fear can never bring about right action, as desire or conflict can never bring about right action. So when you understand fear, the root of fear, go down to the very depths of fear, then the pressure on the brain doesn't exist. Therefore, the brain again becomes fresh, innocent, not something jaded, moulded, shaped, made ugly, as it is now.

So please, if you have not understood this now, spend an hour with yourself, quietly, to find out. You may cry, you may sigh, you may shed tears, but find out how to live without a shadow of fear. Then you will know what love is.

# Brockwood Park, 1 September 1979

THERE ARE THE fears that are deeply hidden, of which you are not conscious, and the obvious psychological and physical fears. There is fear of insecurity, of not having jobs, or having jobs, being frightened to lose them, of the various forms of strikes that are going on, and so on and so on. So most of us are rather nervous, frightened of not being completely physically secure. Obviously, but why? Is it because we are always isolating ourselves as a nation, as a family, as a group? Is this slow process of isolation—the French isolating themselves, also the Germans, and so on—gradually bringing about insecurity for all of us? Can we observe this, not only outwardly? By observing what is happening outwardly, knowing exactly what is going on, from there we can begin to investigate in ourselves. Otherwise we have no criteria; otherwise we deceive ourselves. So we must begin from the outer and work towards the inner. It is like a tide that is going out and coming in. It is not a fixed tide, it is moving out and in all the time.

This isolation, which has been the tribal expression of every human being, is bringing about physical lack of security. If one sees the truth of it as a fact, and not the verbal explanation or the intellectual acceptance of an idea, then one doesn't belong to any group, to any nation, to any culture, to any organized religion, because they are all so separative—the Catholic, the Protestant, the Hindu, and so on. Will you do that, as we are discussing together? Will you drop the things that are false, that are not factual, that have no value whatsoever? Though we think they have value, when you observe, nationality actually breeds wars. So can we drop that so that physically we can bring about a unity of man? And this unity can come about only through religion, not the phoney religions that we have. I hope I am not offending anybody. The Catholic, the Protestant, the Hindu, the Muslim religions are based on thought, put together by thought. And that which thought has created is not sacred, it is just thought, it is just an idea. And you project an idea, symbolize it, then worship it. In that symbol, or in that image, or in that ritual, there is absolutely nothing sacred. And if one actually observes this, then one is free from it to find out what true religion is, because that may bring us together.

So, we can go into much deeper levels of fear, which are psychological fears. Psychological fears in our relationships, psychological fears with regard to the future, fears of the past—that is, fears of time. Please, I am not a professor, a scholar delivering a sermon and then going back to his rotten life. This is something that is very, very serious, which affects all our lives, so please give it your attention and care. There are fears in relationship, fears of uncertainty, fears of the past and the future, fears of not knowing, fears of death, fears of loneliness, the agonizing sense of solitude: You may be related to others, you may have a great many friends, you may be married, you may have children, but there is this sense of deep isolation, this sense of loneliness. That is one of the factors of fear.

There is also the fear of not being able to fulfil. And the desire to fulfil brings with it the sense of frustration, and in that there is fear. There is fear of not being able to be absolutely clear about everything. So there are many, many forms of fear. You can observe your own particular fear, if you are interested, if you are serious. Because a mind that is frightened, knowingly or unknowingly, can try to meditate, but that meditation only leads to further misery, further corruption, because a mind that is frightened can never see what truth is. We are going to find out if it is possible to be totally, completely, free of fear in all its depth.

You know we are undertaking a job that demands a very careful observation: to observe one's own fear. And how you observe that fear is all important. How do you observe it? Is it a fear that you have remembered, and so recall and then look at? Or is it a fear that you have had no time to observe and is therefore still present? Or is the mind unwilling to look at fear? Which is it that is actually happening? Are we unwilling to look, to observe our own fears because most of us do not know how to resolve them? Either we escape, run away, or analyse, thinking thereby we will get rid of a fear, but the fear is still there. So it is important to find out how we look at that fear.

How do we observe fear? This is not a silly question because either you observe it after it has happened or you observe it as it is happening. For most of us, the observation takes place after it has happened. Now, we are asking whether it is possible to observe fear as it arises. That is, you are threatened by another belief. You hold a belief very strongly, so you are frightened about this. You have certain beliefs, certain experiences, certain opinions, judgements, and evaluations. When someone is challenging these there is either resistance, building a wall against it, or you are afraid that you are going to be attacked. Now, can you observe that fear as it arises? Are you doing it? How do you observe that fear? There is the recognition of the response that you call fear— because you had that fear previously, the memory of it is stored up, and when the fear arises you recognize it, right? So you are not observing but recognizing.

Recognition doesn't free the mind from fear. It only strengthens the fear. There are two factors in operation. You feel you are different from that fear, and so you can operate on that fear, control it, chase it away, rationalize it, and so on. That is you doing something about that fear, but in that there is a division— the me and the fear—so there is conflict in that division. Whereas, if you observe, that fear is you. You are not different from that fear. If you once grasp the principle that the observer is the observed, that the fact is that the observer is that fear, then there is no division between the observer and the fear.

Then what takes place? Let's first hold it for a minute. As we asked, are we observing fear through the process of memory, which is recognition, naming? From that, the tradition says control it; the tradition says run away from it; the tradition says do something about it so that you are not frightened. So tradition has educated us to say that the 'me' is different from fear. Can you be free of that tradition and observe that fear? Can you observe without the thought that has remembered the reaction that has been called fear in the past? It requires great attention and skill in observation. In observing there is only pure perception, not the interpretation of that perception by thought. Then what is fear? Now I have observed someone threatening the belief that I hold, the experience that I cling to, my saying that I have achieved, and therefore the fear arises. In observing that fear, we have come to the point when you observe without the division.

Now, the next question is: What is fear? Fear of the dark; fear of husband, wife, girl, or whatever; fear, artificial and actual, and so on? What is fear, apart from the word? The word is not the thing. One must recognize this very deeply. The word is not the thing.

So without the word, what is that which we call fear? Or does the word create the fear? The word creates the fear, the word being the recognition of something that has happened before, which we have called fear. The word becomes important. Like the *Englishman*, the *Frenchman*, the *Russian*, the word is tremendously important for most of us. But the word is not the thing. So what is fear apart from its various expressions? What is the root of it? If we can find the root of it then unconscious and conscious fears can be understood. The moment you have a perception of the root, the conscious mind and the unconscious mind have no importance. There is just the perception of it. What is the root of fear? Fear of yesterday, of a thousand yesterdays, fear of tomorrow, and of death. Or the fear of something that has happened in the past. There is no actual fear now. Please understand this carefully. If suddenly death strikes one, it is finished. It is over. You have a heart attack and it is finished. But the idea that a heart attack might happen in the future is fear. Is the root of fear time, time being a movement of the past, modified in the present, and going on in the future? Is this whole movement the cause of fear, the root of it?

We are asking if thought, which is time, is the root of fear. Thought is movement. Any movement is time. Is the root of fear time? Thought? And can we understand the whole movement of time, psychologically as well as physically? Psychological time is the tomorrow, and so is tomorrow the root of fear? Which means we are talking about daily living not just theories. Can one live without tomorrow? Do it. That is, if you had a physical pain yesterday, to finish with that pain yesterday, and not carry it over to today and into tomorrow. It is the carrying over which is the time that brings fear.

It is totally possible that psychological fear can end if you apply what is being said. The cook can make a marvellous dish but if you are not hungry, if you don't eat it, then it merely remains on the menu and is of no value. But if you eat it, apply it, go into it for yourself, you will see that psychological fear can absolutely come to an end, so that the mind is free from this terrible burden man has carried.

# Brockwood Park, 26 August 1984

HAVE YOU EVER held fear? Do you hold it, not move away from it; not try to suppress or transcend it, or do all kinds of things with it, but just see the depth of fear, and its extraordinary subtleties? And you can only be aware of all that when you are looking at fear without any motive, without trying to do a thing about it, just watching it.

# *From* The Flight of the Eagle
## *London, 16 March 1969*

For MOST OF us, freedom is an idea and not an actuality. When we talk about freedom, we want to be free outwardly, to do what we like, to travel, to be free to express ourselves in different ways, free to think what we like. The outward expression of freedom seems to be extraordinarily important, especially in countries where there is tyranny, dictatorship; and in those countries where outward freedom is possible one seeks more and more pleasure, more and more possessions.

If we are to inquire deeply into what freedom implies, to be inwardly, completely, and totally free—which then expresses itself outwardly in society, in relationship—then we must ask, it seems to me, whether the human mind, heavily conditioned as it is, can ever be free at all. Must it always live and function within the frontiers of its own conditioning, so that there is no possibility of freedom at all? One sees that the mind, verbally understanding that there is no freedom here on this earth, inwardly or outwardly, then begins to invent freedom in another world, a future liberation, heaven, and so on.

Put aside all theoretical, ideological, concepts of freedom so that we can inquire whether our minds, yours and mine, can ever be actually free, free from dependence, free from fear, anxiety, and free from the innumerable problems, both the conscious as well as those at the deeper layers of the unconscious. Can there be complete psychological freedom, so that the human mind can come upon something that is not of time, that is not put together by thought, yet which is not an escape from the actual realities of daily existence?

Unless the human mind is inwardly, psychologically, totally free it is not possible to see what is true, to see if there is a reality not invented by fear, not shaped by the society or the culture in which we live, and which is not an escape from the daily monotony, with its boredom, loneliness, despair, and anxiety. To find out if there is actually such freedom one must be aware of one's own conditioning, of the problems, of the monotonous shallowness, emptiness, insufficiency of one's daily life, and above all one must be aware of fear. One must be aware of oneself neither introspectively nor analytically, but actually be aware of oneself as one is and see if it is at all possible to be entirely free of all those issues that seem to clog the mind.

To explore, as we are going to do, there must be freedom, not at the end, but right at the beginning. Unless one is free one cannot explore, investigate, or examine. To look deeply there needs to be not only freedom, but the discipline that is necessary to observe; freedom and discipline go together—not that one must be disciplined in order to be free. We are using the word *discipline* not in the accepted, traditional sense, which is to conform, imitate, suppress, follow a set pattern; but rather as the root meaning of that word, which is 'to learn'. Learning and freedom go together, freedom bringing its own discipline—not a discipline imposed by the mind in order to achieve a certain result. These two things are essential: freedom and the act of learning. One cannot learn about oneself unless one is free, free so that one can observe, not according to any pattern, formula or concept, but actually observe oneself as one is. That observation, that perception, that seeing, brings about its own discipline and learning; in that there is no conforming, imitation, suppression, or control whatsoever—and in that there is great beauty.

Our minds are conditioned, that is an obvious fact—conditioned by a particular culture or society; influenced by various impressions; by the strains and stresses of relationships; by economic, climatic, educational factors; by religious conformity, and so on. Our minds are trained to accept fear and to escape, if we can, from that fear, never being able to resolve, totally and completely, the whole nature and structure of fear. So our first question is: Can the mind, so heavily burdened, resolve completely, not only its conditioning, but also its fears? Because it is fear that makes us accept conditioning.

Do not merely hear a lot of words and ideas, which are really of no value at all—but through the act of listening, observing your own states of mind, both verbally and nonverbally, simply inquire whether the mind can ever be free—not accepting fear, not escaping, not saying, 'I must develop courage, resistance,' but actually being fully aware of the fear in which one is trapped. Unless one is free from this quality of fear one cannot see very clearly, deeply; and obviously, when there is fear there is no love.

So, can the mind actually ever be free of fear? That seems to me to be—for any person who is at all serious—one of the most primary and essential questions that must be asked and resolved. There are physical fears and psychological fears. The physical fears of pain and the psychological fears, such as memory of having had pain in the past, and the idea of the repetition of that pain in the future; also, the fears of old age, death, the fears of physical insecurity, the fears of the uncertainty of tomorrow, the fears of not being able to be a great success, not being able to achieve, of not being somebody in this rather ugly world; the fears of destruction, the fears of loneliness, of not being able to love or be loved, and so on; the conscious fears as well as the unconscious fears. Can the mind be free, totally, of all this? If the mind says it cannot, then it has made itself incapable, it has distorted itself and is incapable of perception, of understanding, incapable of being completely silent, quiet; it is like a mind in the dark, seeking light and never finding it, and therefore inventing a light of words, concepts, theories.

How is a mind so heavily burdened with fear, with all its conditioning, ever to be free of it? Or must we accept fear as an inevitable thing of life?—and most of us do accept it, put up with it. What shall we do? How shall I, the human being, you as the human being, be rid of this fear? Not be rid of a particular fear, but of the total fear, the whole nature and structure of fear?

What is fear? Don't accept, if I may suggest, what the speaker is saying; the speaker has no authority whatsoever, he is not a teacher, he is not a guru; because if he is a teacher, then you are the follower, and if you are the follower you destroy yourself as well as the teacher. We are trying to find out the truth of this question of fear so completely that the mind is never afraid, and therefore free of all dependence on another, inwardly, psychologically. The beauty of freedom is that you do not leave a mark. The eagle in its flight does not leave a mark; the scientist does. Inquiring into this question of freedom there must be, not only the scientific observation, but also the flight of the eagle that does not leave a mark at all; both are required; there must be both the verbal explanation and the nonverbal perception—for the description is never the actuality that is described; the explanation is obviously never the thing that is explained; the word is never the thing.

If all this is very clear then we can proceed; we can find out for ourselves—not through the speaker, not through his words, not through his ideas or thoughts—whether the mind can be completely free from fear.

The first part is not an introduction; if you have not heard it clearly and understood it, you cannot go on to the next.

To inquire there must be freedom to look; there must be freedom from conclusions, concepts, ideals, prejudices, so that you can observe actually for yourself what fear is. And when you observe very closely, is there fear at all? That is, you can observe very, very closely, intimately, what fear is only when the observer is the observed. We are going to go into that. So what is fear? How does it come about? The obvious physical fears can be understood, like the physical dangers, to which there is instant response; they are fairly easy to understand; we need not go into them too much. But we are talking about psychological fears; how do these psychological fears arise? What is their origin? That is the issue. There is the fear of something that happened yesterday; the fear of something that might happen later on today or tomorrow. There is the fear of what we have known, and there is the fear of the unknown, which is tomorrow. One can see for oneself very clearly that fear arises through the structure of thought—through thinking about that which happened yesterday of which one is afraid, or through thinking about the future, right? Thought breeds fear, doesn't it? Please let us be quite sure; do not accept what the speaker is saying; be absolutely sure for yourself as to whether thought is the origin of fear. Thinking about the pain, the psychological pain that one had some time ago and not wanting it repeated, not wanting to have that thing recalled, thinking about all this, breeds fear. Can we go on from there? Unless we see this very clearly we will not be able to go any further. Thought, thinking about an incident, an experience, a state, in which there has been a disturbance, danger, grief or pain, brings about fear. And thought, having established a certain security, psychologically, does not want that security to be disturbed; any disturbance is a danger and therefore there is fear.

Thought is responsible for fear; also, thought is responsible for pleasure. One has had a happy experience; thought thinks about it and wants it perpetuated. When that is not possible there is a resistance, anger, despair, and fear. So thought is responsible for fear as well as pleasure, isn't it? This is not a verbal conclusion; this is not a formula for avoiding fear. That is, where there is pleasure there is pain and fear perpetuated by thought; pleasure goes with pain, the two are indivisible, and thought is responsible for both. If there were no tomorrow, no next moment about which to think in terms of either fear or pleasure, then neither would exist. Shall we go on from there? Is it an actuality, not as an idea, but a thing that you yourself have discovered and which is therefore real, so you can say, 'I've found out that thought breeds both pleasure and fear'? You have had sexual enjoyment, pleasure; later you think about it in the imagery, the pictures of thinking, and the very thinking about it gives strength to that pleasure, which is now in the imagery of thought, and when that is thwarted there is pain, anxiety, fear, jealousy, annoyance, anger, brutality. And we are not saying that you must not have pleasure.

Bliss is not pleasure; ecstasy is not brought about by thought; it is an entirely different thing. You can come upon bliss or ecstasy only when you understand the nature of thought, which breeds both pleasure and fear.

So the question arises: Can one stop thought? If thought breeds fear and pleasure—for where there is pleasure there must be pain, which is fairly obvious—then one asks oneself: Can thought come to an end?—which does not mean the ending of the perception of beauty, the enjoyment of beauty. It is like seeing the beauty of a cloud or a tree and enjoying it totally, completely, fully; but when thought seeks to have that same experience tomorrow, that same delight that it had yesterday seeing that cloud, that tree, that flower, the face of that beautiful person, then it invites disappointment, pain, fear, and pleasure.

So can thought come to an end? Or is that a wrong question altogether? It is a wrong question because we want to experience an ecstasy, a bliss, which is not pleasure. By ending thought we hope we shall come upon something that is immense, that is not the product of pleasure and fear. Ask what place has thought in life, not how is thought to be ended? What is the relationship of thought to action and to inaction?

What is the relationship of thought to action where action is necessary? Why, when there is complete enjoyment of beauty, does thought come into existence at all? For if it did not, then it would not be carried over to tomorrow. I want to find out—when there is complete enjoyment of the beauty of a mountain, of a beautiful face, a sheet of water—why thought should come there and give a twist to it and say, 'I must have that pleasure again tomorrow'. I have to find out what the relationship of thought is in action; and to find out if thought need interfere when there is no need of thought at all. I see a beautiful tree, without a single leaf, against the sky; it is extraordinarily beautiful and that is enough— finished. Why should thought come in and say, 'I must have that same delight tomorrow'? And I also see that thought must operate in action. Skill in action is also skill in thought. So, what is the actual relationship between thought and action? As it is, our action is based on concepts, on ideas. I have an idea or concept of what should be done and what is done is approximation to that concept, idea, to that ideal. So there is a division between action and the concept, the ideal, the 'should be'; in this division there is conflict. Any division, psychological division, must breed conflict. I am asking myself, 'What is the relationship of thought in action?' If there is division between the action and the idea then action is incomplete. Is there an action in which thought sees something instantly and acts immediately so that there is not an idea, an ideology to be acted on separately? Is there an action in which the very seeing is the action—in which the very thinking is the action? I see that thought breeds fear and pleasure; I see that where there is pleasure there is pain and therefore resistance to pain. I see that very clearly; the seeing of it is the immediate action; in the seeing of it is involved thought, logic, and thinking very clearly; yet the seeing of it is instantaneous and the action is instantaneous—therefore, there is freedom from it.

Are we communicating with each other? Go slowly, it is quite difficult. Please do not say yes so easily. If you say yes, then when you leave the hall, you must be free of fear. Your saying yes is merely an assertion that you have understood verbally, intellectually, which is nothing at all. You and I are here this morning investigating the question of fear, and when you leave the hall there must be complete freedom from it. That means you are a free human being, a different human being, totally transformed—not tomorrow, but now; you see very clearly that thought breeds fear and pleasure; you see that all our values are based on fear and pleasure—moral, ethical, social, religious, spiritual. If you perceive the truth of it—and to see the truth of it you have to be extraordinarily aware, logically, healthily, sanely observing every movement of thought—then that very perception is total action and therefore you are completely out of it; otherwise you will say, 'How am I to be free of fear tomorrow?'

*Questioner:* Is there not spontaneous fear?

*Krishnamurti:* Would you call that fear? When you know fire burns, when you see a precipice, is it fear to jump away from it? When you see a wild animal, a snake, to withdraw, is that fear? Or is it intelligence? That intelligence may be the result of conditioning, because you have been conditioned to the dangers of a precipice, for if you were not you could fall and that would be the end. Your intelligence tells you to be careful; is that intelligence fear? But is it intelligence that operates when we divide ourselves into nationalities, into religious groups? When we make this division between you and me, we and they, is that intelligence? That which is in operation in such division, which brings about danger, which divides people, which brings war, is that intelligence operating or is it fear? There it is fear, not intelligence. In other words, we have fragmented ourselves; part of us acts, where necessary, intelligently, as in avoiding a precipice, or a bus going by; but we are not intelligent enough to see the dangers of nationalism, the dangers of division between people. So one part of us—a very small part of us—is intelligent, the rest of us is not. Where there is fragmentation there must be conflict, there must be misery; the very essence of conflict is the division, the contradiction in us. That contradiction is not to be integrated. It is one of our peculiar idiosyncrasies that we must integrate ourselves. I do not know what it really means. Who is it that is going to integrate the two divided, opposed, natures? For is not the integrator himself part of that division? But when one sees the totality of it, when one has the perception of it, without any choice—there is no division.

# *Madras, 7 January 1979*

IF WE HAVE no relationship with one another, there is fear. One dominates the other, and either they separate or only come together in bed. So we live a brutal life with one another. Don't you have all this? And in what way shall we bring order that is enduring—not order one day and disorder the next day? What brings about this contradiction in relationship? What brings this division between you, your wife or your husband, and your children? Division is disorder. Muslim and Hindu, Jew and Arab, Communism, totalitarianism, and freedom. These opposites are the essence of disorder. So what brings about disorder in our relationships, with the most intimate and the not so intimate? Have you ever thought about it?

# Madras, 1 January 1984

WE OUGHT TO talk over fear together because that is part of our life, probably the major part of our life. What is the cause of fear? Not the object that creates fear, not something the word evokes. You understand? The word may bring about fear, the word *fear* may arouse fear, but when you have no word, but only observe the reaction that you call fear, what is the root of it? This requires a great deal of exploration, and one hopes that you are willing to go into this. Fear is time. I am going to go into it. Fear is a movement in time. So first let us examine carefully what time is. Time as the sun rises and sets; the interval between the sun rising and the sun setting is time. There is time to cover a distance from point to point; there is time for you to go from here to your home. This takes time, whether an instant or an hour. So there is physical time. To learn a language, to learn to drive a car, takes time. If you want to be a pilot, it takes months, and so on. So there is physical time. And also there is psychological time: I will be, I will become; I am a clerk, but I will become the manager one day; I am ignorant, but one day I will be enlightened. That is, I am this, I will be that. That is psychological time.

There is physical or chronological time and there is psychological time, which says, 'I am, but I will not be. I am living, but I will die. That's a tremendous interval. I am fifteen, but I will die one day when I am eighty.' That is the movement of that long interval which is psychological time. And also there is time as the future. I have a job now, but I might lose that job; I am quarreling with my wife, but one day we will be happy together. So there is time as the past, time as the present, and time as the future. In the now, all the past and the future are contained. So the future and the past exist now. I am the result of all the past, modifying itself in the present, and the future is the present. Unless I radically bring about—or rather, unless there is—a mutation in my brain cells, I will be what I am now. So the present is the past and the future, contained now. That is time.

What relationship has time to fear? Most human beings are frightened, have innumerable forms of fear: fear of darkness, fear of dying, fear of living, fear that you might lose what you have, fear of your wife or your husband. There is fear of what you possess, fear of growing old and dying. So human beings throughout the world have tremendous anxiety, which is part of fear: anxiety about not fulfilling, anxiety about not being yourself, anxiety about what other people might do to you, and so on. All that is a form of fear. So what is the relationship between fear and time? And shall we trim the branches of fear, take one branch after another, or shall we deal with the root of fear? Have you understood my question? I may be frightened of my wife, or I may be frightened of darkness, and I want that particular problem solved. But also I have other problems of fear, it is not only one that I have. There is fear that my brain will degenerate, fear that God won't give me what I want unless I go to a particular temple.

So what is the relationship between fear and time? And also, what is the relationship of fear with thought? I am afraid of so many things but I want to understand the root of fear, because if I can understand, see the quality, the nature, the structure of fear, then it is finished. But, if I merely trim the branches, then fear will continue. So our concern is not how to be rid of fear, that's one of our fallacies. But if we can go, delve deeply, into the nature of fear, then we shall be able to be free of it entirely. And if

you investigate it, question, ask yourself, then you might be utterly free of fear, and then there will be no gods. When man is
free of all fear he needs no comfort, he needs no reward, he
doesn't seek something that will help him. Fear is the burden that
mankind has carried for a million years. So let's go into it.

We said time is a factor of fear. There is the remembrance
of an incident that caused fear, which is registered or recorded in
the brain. And that record is still there and I now have fear. So the
record remembers the fact of fear, and from the past I recognize
the fear. The knowledge of a past incident that caused fear is registered in the brain, as on a tape. So the brain has knowledge of
fear. So knowledge is fear. Go into it, see the beauty of it, and then
you will see what it means. When fear arises now, memory steps in
and says, 'Yes, I know that is fear'. Which means the knowledge
that you have had with regard to fear says, 'That is fear'. So knowledge itself becomes fear. And the word *fear* may also contribute to
fear. So knowledge is the word, and the word may cause fear. So
can you look, can there be an observation of fear without the
knowledge of other fears so that there is perception of fear without
the movement of knowledge?

So fear is the movement of knowledge as the past, and
that knowledge is time. So fear is also part of thought: I might die
tomorrow, I might lose my job, I am this but I will become that—
it's all the movement of thought. The 'tomorrow' is time and
thought says, 'I might lose my job'. Thought and time are movements of knowledge. So can the brain not record? You flatter me,
the brain immediately records it. Or you insult me, the brain again
records. It is a machine that is recording all the time. And that becomes our knowledge, and from that knowledge we act. Now if
you flatter me, but the brain does not record, I don't say you are a
great friend of mine. Nor if you insult me is that recorded. Then
knowledge, which might create fear, is not necessary. But I must
have knowledge to write a letter, to do business. If I am an ac-
countant I must have knowledge. But is it possible not to record

psychologically? You understand? Find out whether this is possible—which means the brain has seen the fact of it and therefore is unconditioning itself.

So fear is a movement of time and thought, and that very knowledge prevents us from seeing something new, fresh. Whereas if you can look at fear as it arises for the first time, then it is something entirely different, it's a reaction, a physical and a psychological reaction. So fear, the root of fear, is the movement of time and thought. But if you understand the nature and structure of time, not intellectually but actually, and also of thought—which means to investigate and be completely familiar with the movement of time and thought, which is the basis of fear—then because you are so completely attentive, that very attention burns away fear.

# Conversation with Mary Zimbalist
# Brockwood Park, 5 October 1984

*Mary Zimbalist:* There is a subject you have talked about so many times, but it keeps coming back in people's questions and preoccupations, and that is the subject of fear. Do you want to talk about that?

*Krishnamurti:* It is a rather complicated subject. It really requires a great deal of inquiry because it is so subtle and so varied. And it is actual too, though we make it into an abstraction. There is the actuality of fear and the idea of fear. So we must be very clear what we are talking about. You and I sitting here, at this present moment, are not afraid. There is no sense of apprehension, or danger. At this instant there is no fear.

So fear is both an abstraction—as an idea, as a word—and a fact. First of all let's deal with these two. Why do we generally make an abstraction of things? Why do we see something actual and then turn it into an idea? Is it because the idea is easier to pursue? Or the ideal is our conditioning? Or we are educated to ideas, and not educated to deal with facts? Why is this? Why is it that human beings throughout the world deal with abstractions, with what should be, what must be, what will happen, and so on? There is the whole world of ideation and the ideologies, whether it be the communist ideology based on Marx and Lenin, or the capitalists' ideas of so-called free enterprise, or the whole world of religious concepts, beliefs, ideas, and the theologians working those out. Why is it that ideas, ideals, have become so extraordinarily important? From the ancient Greeks, and even before the Greeks, ideas prevailed. And still ideas, ideals, separate man and bring wars of all kinds. Why do the brains of human beings operate in this way? Is it because they cannot deal with facts directly and so escape subtly into ideations? Ideas are really very divisive factors, they bring friction, they divide communities, nations, sects, religions, and so on. Ideas, beliefs, faith—are all based on thought. And what exactly is a fact, not an opinion about a fact, or opinion made into facts.

*MZ:* What is the fact of fear?

*K:* The actual fear is the fact, not the abstraction of it. If one can move away from the abstraction then we can deal with fact. But if they are both running parallel all the time, then there is a conflict between the two. That is, between the idea, the ideology, dominating the fact, and the fact sometimes dominating the idea.

*MZ:* Most people would say that the fact of fear is the very painful emotion of fear.

*K:* Now let us look at that, not the idea of fear. Let us look at the actual fact of fear, and remain with that fact, which requires a great deal of inward discipline.

*MZ:* Can you describe what remaining with the fact of fear actually is?

*K:* It is like holding a jewel, an intricate pattern by an artist, who has brought this extraordinary jewel. You look at it, you don't condemn it, you don't say, 'How beautiful' and run away with words, but you are looking at this extraordinary thing put together by hand, by cunning fingers and the brain. You are watching it, you are looking at it. You turn it round, look at the various sides, the back and the front and the side, and you never let it go.

*MZ:* Do you mean that you just feel it very acutely, very sensitively, with great care.

*K:* With care, that is what happens.

*MZ:* But you feel it because it is an emotion.

*K:* Of course. You have the feeling of beauty, the feeling of the intricate pattern, and the sparkle, the brightness of the jewels, and so on. So can we deal with the fact of fear and look at it that way, and not escape, not say, 'Well, I don't like fear', get nervous, apprehensive, and suppress or control or deny it, nor move it into another field? We can do all that; just remain with that fear. So fear then becomes an actual fact, which is there, whether you are conscious of it or not. If you have hidden it very, very deeply, it is still there.

So then we can ask, very carefully and hesitantly, what is this fear? Why do human beings, after this tremendous evolution, still live with fear? Is it something that can be operated upon and removed, like a disease, like cancer? Is it something that can be operated upon? Which means there is an entity who can operate upon it. But that very entity is an abstraction of trying to do something about fear. That entity is unreal. What is factual is fear. And it requires very careful attention not to be caught in the abstraction of one who says, 'I am observing fear', or one who says, 'I must put away or control fear', and so on.

So we look at that fear, and in the very act of looking, of watching fear, one begins to discover the origin of fear, and what the causation of fear is. Because the very fact of looking at it is to see how it came about. Not to analyse or dissect. That very close, delicate watching reveals the content of fear, the content being the origin, the beginning, the causation—because where there is a cause there is an end. The cause can never be different from the result. So in the observation, in the watching, the causation is revealed.

*MZ:* The causation that you are speaking of is presumably not an individual fear, a particular fear? You are speaking of the causation of fear itself.

*K:* Fear itself, not the various forms of fear. See how we break up fear. That's part of our tradition, to bring about a fragmentation of fear, and therefore be concerned with only one type of fear. Not with the whole tree of fear, but a particular branch, or a particular leaf of it. The whole nature, the structure, the quality of fear—in observing that very closely, in the very watching there is the revelation of the causation—not you analysing to find out the cause but the very watching showing the causation, which is time and thought. It is simple when you put it that way. Everybody would accept that it is time and thought. If there were no time and thought there would be no fear.

*MZ:* Could you enlarge a little bit on that because most people think that there is something—how can I put it—they don't see that there is no future, they think 'I am afraid now' from a cause, they don't see the factor of time involved.

*K:* I think it is fairly simple. There is time when I say, 'I am afraid because I have done something in the past', or I have had pain in the past, or somebody has hurt me, and I don't want to be hurt anymore. All that is the past, the background, which is time. And there is the future; that is, I am this now, but I will die. Or I might lose my job, or my wife will be angry with me, and so on. So there is this past and the future, and we are caught in between the two. The past has its relationship with the future; the future is not something separate from the past; there is a movement of modification from the past to the future, to tomorrow. So that is time: this movement, which is the past as I have been, and the future as I will be, which is this constant becoming. And that too is another complex problem that may be the causation of fear.

So time is a basic factor of fear. There is no question about it. I have a job now, I have money now, I have a shelter over my head, but tomorrow or many hundred tomorrows might deprive me of all that—some accident, some fire, some lack of insurance. All that is a time factor. And also, thought is a factor of fear. Thought: I have been, I am, but I may not be. Thought is limited because it is based on knowledge. Knowledge is always accumulative and that which is being added to is always limited, so knowledge is limited, so thought is limited; because thought is based on knowledge, memory, and so on.

So thought and time are the central factors of fear. Thought is not separate from time. They are one. These are the facts. This is the causation of fear. It is a fact—not an idea, not an abstraction—that thought and time is the cause of fear. It is singular.

So a man then asks: How do I stop time and thought? Because his intention, his desire, his longing, is to be free from fear. And so he is caught in his own desire to be free but he is not watching the causation, watching very carefully, without any movement. Watching implies a state of the brain in which there is no movement; it is like watching a bird very closely, as we watched a dove this morning on the window sill, all the feathers, the red eyes, the sparkle in the eyes, the beak, the shape of its head, the wings. That which you watch very carefully reveals not only the causation but the ending of the thing that you are watching. So this watching is really most extraordinarily important, not asking how to end thought, or be free from fear, or what is meant by time, and all the complications. We are watching fear without any abstraction, which is the actual now. The now contains all time, which means the present holds the past, the future, and the present. So we can listen to this very carefully, not only with the hearing of the ear, but listen to the word and go beyond the word, see the actual nature of fear, and not just read about fear. Watching becomes so tremendously beautiful, sensitive, alive.

All this requires an extraordinary quality of attention, because in attention there is no activity of the self. The self-interest in our life is the cause of fear. This sense of me and my concern, my happiness, my success, my failure, my achievement, I am this, I am not; this whole self-centred observation, with all its expressions of fear, agony, depression, pain, anxiety, aspiration, and sorrow, all that is self-interest, whether in the name of God, in the name of prayer, or in the name of faith. It is self-interest. Where there is self-interest there must be fear, and all the consequences of fear. Then one asks again: Is it possible to live in this world where self-interest is predominant? In the totalitarian world and the capitalist world self-interest is dominant. In the hierarchical Catholic world and in every religious world, self-interest is dominant. They are perpetuating fear. Though they talk about living with peace on earth, they really don't mean it because self-interest, with the desire for power, position, for fulfilment, and so on, is the factor that is destroying not only the world but the extraordinary capacity of our own brain. The brain has remarkable capacity, as is shown in the extraordinary things they are doing in technology. And we never apply that same immense capacity inwardly, to be free of fear, to end sorrow, to know what is love and compassion, with its intelligence. We never search, explore that field; we are caught by the world with all its misery.

# New Delhi, 1 November 1981

YOU ARE WATCHING the operation of your own brain, the operation of your own mind. You are discovering for yourself the way you think, the way you feel, your fears, of which you must also consider pleasure. Because they are the two sides of the same coin. This whole movement of fear, desire, and time is you. That is what your consciousness is. You can't escape from your consciousness, you are that. So remain with that. When you remain with it, give all your attention to it, like bringing a strong light upon something that is dark, it dispels the whole pattern of fear. And in considering fear we consider pleasure, because pleasure brings also pain and fear. Most of us have always sought pleasure—sexual pleasure, or that of the intellect; the pleasure of devotion, which is romanticism; or the pleasure of popularity, and all that business. We are always seeking pleasure, and ultimate pleasure is, of course, Brahmin, or another invented God. I do not know if you have realized that thought has created God. God hasn't created you to live a miserable life, but we have created god. Thought has created it and we worship that which thought has created, which becomes rather silly.

So we have to examine pleasure. The pleasure of ambition, of possession, of being an ascetic, of sex. What is pleasure? Why has man pursued it? What is the movement of pleasure? You see a beautiful sunset, with its light and glory. A great light across the heavens, the beauty, the delight of something incredible. If you have ever looked at a sunset with all your heart and brain and mind, it is an extraordinary sight, as is the sight of an early morning. The other day we saw the sun rise. There was the waning moon and the morning star, clear light on the waters, and the snow-covered hills, and there was great beauty, which no painter, no poet, could describe. There was a delight in that. That delight is recorded in the brain. Then that pleasure is remembered and we want that pleasure to be repeated. The repetition is no longer pleasure; it becomes memory as pleasure. It is not the original perception of that waning moon, the clear sky with that low, single star and the beauty of that light on the water. That remembrance is pleasure; it was not at the moment of perception. At the moment of seeing there was no pleasure; there was that. But it has been recorded, then there is the remembrance of that, and that pleasure is the remembrance. And there is the demand for that pleasure to be repeated.

At the moment when you see the beauty of a mountain, with the snow, with the clear, blue sky, there is no pleasure, there is only that immensity, that grandeur, that majesty; later on pleasure begins when you want it to be repeated, which means the remembrance, thought, time; the same thing as fear. I have seen the whole movement of that thing that has happened yesterday morning and that I want it again. It is exactly the same movement as fear and pleasure. So our minds, our existences, are caught between these two, reward and punishment. That is our life. That is me, you, the self, that lives, has its root in this time, thought, pleasure, fear, reward, and punishment. Heaven is there if you do the right thing, if you don't you go to hell! The same thing repeated over and over again.

So is what has been said an abstraction as an idea? Or do you see for yourself how your mind is working, how your brain is operating? Do you see the truth that thought, time, is the root of fear just as it is the root of pleasure? So they are both the same. You discover fear is pleasure. Have you seen the truth of this so that you are free of fear? Then there is freedom, then you have strength, vitality to fight all this ugliness in the world.

# Ojai, 12 May 1981

*Questioner:* How does one tackle the dormant seed of fear within one? You have talked of fear several times, but it is neither possible to face fear nor to uproot it. Is it that there is another factor that operates to dissolve it? Can one do anything about it?

*Krishnamurti:* The questioner asks if there is another factor that will dissolve, uproot the very root of fear. Can we go into it together and investigate a very serious and complex problem? This fear has been with humanity since time immemorial, and apparently they have not solved it. We carry, day after day until we almost die, this burden of fear. Can that fear be totally uprooted? The questioner says, one has tried several different ways but somehow it doesn't disappear. Is there another factor that will help to uproot it?

Can we look at our fear, not only our physical fears but those of loss, of insecurity, the fear of losing one's children, that sense of insecurity when there is divorce; the fear of not achieving something? There are various forms of fear. Fear of not being loved, fear of loneliness, fear of what happens after death, fear of heaven and hell—you know all that kind of stuff. One is frightened of so many things. Now can we, each one of us, consciously, sensitively be aware of our own fear? Do we know our own fear? It may be losing a job, not having money, death, and so on. Can we look at it first, not to try to dissolve it, or conquer it, or go beyond it, but just to observe it? Consciously observe the fears, or one fear, that one has? And there are dormant fears that are deep-rooted, unconscious, way down in the recesses of one's mind. Can those dormant fears be awakened and looked at now? Or must they appear only in a crisis, in a shock, in certain strong challenges? Can one awaken the whole structure of fear? Not only the conscious fears but also the fears that have collected in the unconscious, shadowy recesses of one's brain? Can we do that?

First, can we look at our fear? And how do we look at it? How do we face it? Suppose I am frightened that I cannot be saved except by some divine person. There is a deep-rooted fear of two thousand years. I am not even observing that fear. It is part of my tradition, part of my conditioning that I can't do anything, but that somebody else, an outside agency, is going to help me, save me. Save me; I don't know from what, but it doesn't matter! And that is part of one's fear. And of course there is the fear of death. That is the ultimate fear. Can I observe a particular fear that I have, and not guide it, shape it, overcome it, try to rationalize it? Can I look at it? And how do I observe it? Do I observe it as an outsider looking in, or do I observe it as part of me? Fear is not separate from my consciousness, something outside of me. Fear is part of me. Obviously. So can I observe that fear without the division of the observer and the observed?

Can I observe fear without the division that thought has created between fear and the entity that says, 'I must face fear'? Just observe fear without that division? Is that possible? You see, our conditioning, our training, our education, our religious ambitions, all point out that the two are separate—the me is different from that which is not me. We never recognize or accept the fact that violence is not separate from us. I think that may be one of the factors why we are not able to be free of fear, because we are always operating on fear. We are always saying to ourselves, 'I must get rid of it', 'What am I to do with it?' All the rationalization, inquiries, as though fear is something separate from the inquirer, from the person who inquires into fear.

So can we observe fear without that division? That is, the word *fear* is not fear. And also see whether the word creates the fear—like the word *Communist* to many people is a frightening word. So can we look at that thing called fear without the word, and also find out if the word is creating the fear?

Then is there another factor, which is not mere observation, but bringing, or having, energy that will dissipate that fear, having such tremendous energy that fear doesn't exist. You understand? Is fear a matter of lack of energy, lack of attention? And if it is a lack of energy, how does one come naturally to have this tremendous vitality, energy, that pushes fear away altogether?

Energy may be the factor that will have no sense of fear. You see, most of us dissipate our energy in constant occupation with something or other: if you are a housewife, a businessman, a scientist, a careerist, you are always occupied. And such occupation may be, and is, I think, a dissipation of energy. Like the man who is perpetually occupied about meditation, perpetually occupied with whether there is God. You know, various forms of occupation. Is not such occupation, worry, concern, a waste of energy? If one is afraid and says, 'I must not be afraid, what am I to do?' and so on, it is another kind of occupation. It is only a mind that is free from occupation of any kind that has tremendous energy. That may be one of the factors that may dissipate fear.

# *From* Krishnamurti's Notebook
## *Paris, September 1961*

### September 14

THERE IS FEAR. Fear is never an actuality; it is either before or after the active present. When there is fear in the active present, is it fear? It is there and there is no escape from it, no evasion possible. There, at that actual moment, there is total attention at the moment of danger, physical or psychological. When there is complete attention there is no fear. But the actual fact of inattention breeds fear; fear arises when there is an avoidance of the fact, a flight; then the very escape itself is fear.

    Fear and its many forms—guilt, anxiety, hope, despair— is there in every movement of relationship; it is there in every search for security; it is there in so-called love and worship; it is there in ambition and success; it is there in life and in death; it is there in physical things and in psychological factors. There is fear in so many forms and at all the levels of our consciousness. Defence, resistance, and denial spring from fear. Fear of the dark and fear of light; fear of going and fear of coming. Fear begins and ends with the desire to be secure; inward and outward security, with the desire to be certain, to have permanency. The continuity of permanence is sought in every direction, in virtue, in relationship, in action, in experience, in knowledge, in outward and inward things. To find security and be secure is the everlasting cry. It is this insistent demand that breeds fear.

But is there permanency, outwardly or inwardly? Perhaps in a measure, outwardly, there might be, and even that is precarious; wars, revolutions, progress, accident, and earthquakes. There must be food, clothes, and shelter; that is essential and necessary for all. Though it is sought after, blindly and with reason, is there ever inward certainty, inward continuity, permanency? There is not. The flight from this reality is fear. The incapacity to face this reality breeds every form of hope and despair.

Thought itself is the source of fear. Thought is time; thought of tomorrow is pleasure or pain; if it's pleasurable, thought will pursue it, fearing its end; if it's painful, the very avoidance of it is fear. Both pleasure and pain cause fear. Time as thought and time as feeling bring fear. It is the understanding of thought, the mechanism of memory and experience, that is the ending of fear. Thought is the whole process of consciousness, the open and the hidden; thought is not merely the thing thought upon but the origin of itself. Thought is not merely belief, dogma, idea, and reason; but the centre from which these arise. This centre is the origin of all fear. But is there the experiencing of fear or is there the awareness of the cause of fear from which thought is taking flight? Physical self-protection is sane, normal, and healthy; but every other form of self-protection, inwardly, is resistance and it always gathers, builds up strength, which is fear. But this inward fear makes outward security a problem of class, prestige, power, and so there is competitive ruthlessness.

When this whole process of thought, time, and fear is seen, not as an idea, an intellectual formula, then there is total ending of fear, conscious or hidden. Self-understanding is the awakening and ending of fear.

And when fear ceases, then the power to breed illusion, myth, and visions, with their hope and despair, also ceases, and then only begins a movement of going beyond consciousness, which is thought and feeling. It is the emptying of the innermost recesses and deep hidden wants and desires. Then when there is this total emptiness, when there is absolutely and literally nothing, no influence, no value, no frontier, no word, then in that complete stillness of time-space, there is that which is unnameable.

## September 15

It was a lovely evening, the sky was clear and in spite of city light, the stars were brilliant; though the tower was flooded with light from all sides, one could see the distant horizon and down below patches of light were on the river; though there was the everlasting roar of traffic, it was a peaceful evening. Meditation crept up on one like a wave covering the sands. It was not a meditation that the brain could capture in its net of memory; it was something to which the total brain yielded without any resistance. It was a meditation that went far beyond any formula, method; method and formula and repetition destroy meditation. In its movement it took everything in, the stars, the noise, the quiet and the stretch of water. But there was no meditator; the meditator, the observer, must cease for meditation to be. The breaking up of the meditator is also meditation; but when the meditator ceases then there's an altogether different meditation.

It was very early in the morning; Orion was coming up over the horizon and the Pleiades were nearly overhead. The roar of the city had quietened and at that hour there were no lights in any of the windows and there was a pleasant, cool breeze. In complete attention there is no experiencing. In inattention there is; it is this inattention that gathers experience, multiplying memory, building walls of resistance; it is this inattention that builds up the self-centred activities. Inattention is concentration, which is exclusion, a cutting off; concentration knows distraction and the endless conflict of control and discipline. In the state of inattention, every response to any challenge is inadequate; this inadequacy is experience. Experience makes for insensitivity; dulls the mechanism of thought; thickens the walls of memory, and habit, routine, become the norm. Experience, inattention, is not liberating. Inattention is slow decay.

In complete attention there is no experiencing; there's no centre which experiences, nor a periphery within which experience can take place. Attention is not concentration, which is narrowing, limiting. Total attention includes, never excludes. Superficiality of attention is inattention; total attention includes the superficial and the hidden, the past and its influence on the present, moving into the future. All consciousness is partial, confined, and total attention includes consciousness, with its limitations and so is able to break down the borders, the limitations. All thought is conditioned and thought cannot uncondition itself. Thought is time and experience; it is essentially the result of non-attention.

What brings about total attention? Not any method nor any system; they bring about a result, promised by them. But total attention is not a result, any more than love is; it cannot be induced, it cannot be brought about by any action. Total attention is the negation of the results of inattention, but this negation is not the act of knowing attention. What is false must be denied not because you already know what is true; if you knew what is true, the false would not exist. The true is not the opposite of the false; love is not the opposite of hate. Because you know hate, you do not know love. Denial of the false, denial of the things of non-attention, is not the outcome of the desire to achieve total attention. Seeing the false as the false and the true as the true and the true in the false is not the result of comparison. To see the false as the false is attention. The false as the false cannot be seen when there is opinion, judgement, evaluation, attachment, and so on, which are the result of non-attention. Seeing the whole fabric of non-attention is total attention. An attentive mind is an empty mind.

The purity of the otherness is its immense and impenetrable strength. And it was there with extraordinary stillness this morning.

September 16

It was a clear, bright evening; there wasn't a cloud. It was
so lovely that it was surprising that such an evening should happen in a town. The moon was between the arches of the tower
and the whole setting seemed so artificial and unreal. The air was
so soft and pleasant that it might have been a summer's evening.
On the balcony it was very quiet and every thought had subsided
and meditation seemed a casual movement, without any direction. But there was, though. It began nowhere and went on into
vast, unfathomable emptiness where the essence of everything is.
In this emptiness there is an expanding, exploding movement
whose very explosion is creation and destruction. Love is the
essence of this destruction.

Either we seek through fear, or being free from it we
seek without any motive. This search does not spring from discontent; not being satisfied with every form of thought and feeling, seeing their significance, is not discontent. Discontent is so
easily satisfied when thought and feeling have found some form
of shelter, success, a gratifying position, a belief, and so on, only to
be roused again when that shelter is attacked, shaken, or broken
down. With this cycle most of us are familiar—hope and despair.
Search, whose motive is discontent, can only lead to some form of
illusion, a collective or a private illusion, a prison of many attrac-
tions. But there is a seeking without any motive whatsoever; then
is it a seeking? Seeking implies, does it not, an objective, an end
already known or felt or formulated. If it's formulated it's the cal-
culation of thought, putting together all the things it has known or
experienced; to find what is sought after methods and systems are
devised. This is not seeking at all; it is merely a desire to gain a
gratifying end or merely to escape into some fancy or promise of a
theory or belief. This is not seeking. When fear, satisfaction, escape, have lost their significance, then is there seeking at all?

If the motive of all search has withered away—discontent
and the urge to succeed are dead—is there seeking? If there is no

seeking, will consciousness decay, become stagnant? On the contrary, it is this seeking, going from one commitment to another, from one church to another, that weakens that essential energy to understand what is. The *what is* is ever new; it has never been and it will never be. The release of this energy is only possible when every form of search ceases.

## September 17

It had been a hot, smothering day and even the pigeons were hiding and the air was hot, and in a city it was not at all pleasant. It was a cool night and the few stars that were visible were bright, even the city lights couldn't dim them. They were there with amazing intensity.

It was a day of the otherness; it went on quietly all day and at moments it flared up, became very intense and became quiet again, to go on quietly. It was there with such intensity that all movement became impossible; one was forced to sit down. On waking in the middle of the night it was there with great force and energy. On the terrace, with the roar of the city not so insistent, every form of meditation became inadequate and unnecessary for it was there in full measure. It's a benediction and everything seems rather silly and infantile. On these occasions, the brain is always very quiet but in no way asleep and the whole of the body becomes motionless. It is a strange affair.

How little one changes. Through some form of compulsion, pressure, outward and inner, one changes, which is really an adjustment. Some influence, a word, a gesture, makes one change the pattern of habit but not very much. Propaganda, a newspaper, an incident does alter, to some extent, the course of life. Fear and reward break down the habit of thought only to reform into another pattern. A new invention, a new ambition, a new belief, does bring about certain changes. But all these changes are on the surface, like strong wind on water; they are not fundamental, deep, devastating. All change that comes through motive is no change at all. Economic, social revolution is a reaction and any change brought about through reaction is not a radical change; it is only a change in pattern. Such change is merely adjustment, a mechanical affair of desire for comfort, security, mere physical survival.

Then what brings about fundamental mutation? Consciousness, the open and the hidden, the whole machinery of thought, feeling, experience, is within the borders of time and space. It is an indivisible whole; the division, conscious and hidden, is there only for the convenience of communication but the division is not factual. The upper level of consciousness can and does modify itself, adjust itself, change itself, reform itself, acquire new knowledge, technique; it can change itself to conform to a new social, economic pattern but such changes are superficial and brittle. The unconscious, the hidden, can and does intimate and hint through dreams its compulsions, its demands, its stored-up desires. Dreams need interpretations but the interpreter is always conditioned. There is no need for dreams if during the waking hours there is a choiceless awareness in which every fleeting thought and feeling is understood; then sleep has altogether a different meaning. Analysis of the hidden implies the observer and the observed, the censor and the thing that is judged. In this there is not only conflict but the observer himself is conditioned and his evaluation, interpretation, can never be true; it will be crooked, perverted. So self-analysis or an analysis by another, however professional, may bring about some superficial changes, an adjustment in relationship and so on, but analysis will not bring about a radical transformation of consciousness. Analysis does not transform consciousness.

### September 18

The late afternoon sun was on the river and among the russet leaves of autumnal trees along the long avenue; the colours were burning intensely and of such variety; the narrow water was aflame. A long queue was waiting along the wharf to take the pleasure boat and the cars were making an awful noise. On a hot day the big town was almost unbearable; the sky was clear and the sun was without mercy. But very early this morning when Orion was overhead and only one or two cars passed along the river, there was on the terrace quietness and meditation with a complete openness of mind and heart, verging on death. To be completely open, to be utterly vulnerable, is death. Death then has no corner to take shelter; only in the shade, in the secret recesses of thought and desire, there is death. But death is always there to a heart that has withered in fear and hope; is always there where thought is waiting and watching. In the park an owl was hooting and it was a pleasant sound, clear and so early; it came and went with varied intervals and it seemed to like its own voice, for not another replied.

Meditation breaks down the frontiers of consciousness; it breaks down the mechanism of thought and the feeling that thought arouses. Meditation caught in a method, in a system of rewards and promises, cripples and tames energy. Meditation is the freeing of energy in abundance; and control, discipline, and suppression spoil the purity of that energy. Meditation is the flame burning intensely without leaving any ashes. Words, feeling, thought, always leave ashes and to live on ashes is the way of the world. Meditation is danger for it destroys everything, nothing whatsoever is left, not even a whisper of desire, and in this vast, unfathomable emptiness there is creation and love.

To continue—analysis, personal or professional, does not bring about mutation of consciousness. No effort can transform it; effort is conflict and conflict only strengthens the walls of consciousness. No reason, however logical and sane, can liberate consciousness, for reason is idea wrought by influence, experience, and knowledge, and all these are the children of consciousness. When all this is seen as false, a false approach to mutation, the denial of the false is the emptying of consciousness. Truth has no opposite nor has love; the pursuit of the opposite does not lead to truth, only the denial of the opposite. There is no denial if it is the outcome of hope or of attaining. There is denial only when there is no reward or exchange. There is renunciation only when there is no gain in the act of renouncing. Denial of the false is the freedom from the positive; the positive with its opposite. The positive is authority with its acceptance, conformity, imitation, and experience with its knowledge.

To deny is to be alone; alone from all influence, tradition, and need, with its dependence and attachment. To be alone is to deny the conditioning, the background. The frame in which consciousness exists and has its being is its conditioning; to be choicelessly aware of this conditioning, and the total denial of it, is to be alone. This aloneness is not isolation, loneliness, self-enclosing occupation. Aloneness is not withdrawal from life; on the contrary it is the total freedom from conflict and sorrow, from fear and death. This aloneness is the mutation of consciousness; complete transformation of what has been. This aloneness is emptiness, it is not the positive state of being, nor the not being. It is emptiness; in this fire of emptiness the mind is made young, fresh, and innocent. It is innocency alone that can receive the timeless, the new, which is ever destroying itself. Destruction is creation. Without love, there is no destruction.

Beyond the enormous sprawling town were the fields, woods, and hills.

### September 19

Is there a future? There is a tomorrow, already planned; certain things that have to be done; there is also the day after tomorrow, with all the things that are to be done; next week and next year. These cannot be altered, perhaps modified or changed altogether, but the many tomorrows are there; they cannot be denied. And there is space, from here to there, near and far; the distance in kilometres; space between entities; the distance that thought covers in a flash; the other side of the river and the distant moon. Time to cover space, distance, and time to cross over the river; from here to there, time is necessary to cover that space, it may take a minute, a day, or a year. This time is by the sun and by the watch, time is a means to arrive. This is fairly simple and clear. Is there a future apart from this mechanical, chronological time? Is there an arriving, is there an end for which time is necessary?

The pigeons were on the roof, so early in the morning; they were cooing, preening, and pursuing each other. The sun wasn't up yet and there were a few vaporous clouds, scattered all over the sky; they had no colour yet and the roar of traffic had not yet begun. There was plenty of time yet for the usual noises to begin and beyond all these walls were the gardens. In the evening yesterday, the grass where no one is allowed to walk—except, of course, the pigeons and a few sparrows—was very green, startlingly green, and the flowers were very bright. Everywhere else was man with his activities and interminable work. There was the tower, so strongly and delicately put together, and presently it would be flooded with brilliant light. The grass seemed so perishable and the flowers would fade, for autumn was everywhere. But long before the pigeons were on the roof, on the terrace, meditation was gladness. There was no reason for this ecstasy—to have a cause for joy is no longer joy; it was simply there and thought could not capture it and make it into a remembrance. It was too strong and active for thought to play with it and thought and feeling became very quiet and still. It came wave upon wave, a living thing that nothing could contain and with this joy there was benediction. It was all so utterly beyond all thought and demand. Is there an arriving? To arrive is to be in sorrow and within the shadow of fear. Is there an arriving inwardly, a goal to be reached, an end to be gained? Thought has fixed an end, God, bliss, success, virtue, and so on. But thought is only a reaction; a response of memory and thought breeds time to cover the space between what is and what should be. The what should be, the ideal, is verbal, theoretical; it has no reality. The actual has no time; it has no end to achieve, no distance to travel. The fact is and everything else is not. There is no fact if there's not death to ideal, to achievement, to an end; the ideal, the goal, are an escape from the fact. The fact has no time and no space. And then is there death? There is a withering away; the machinery of the physical organism deteriorates, gets worn out, which is death. But that is inevitable, as the lead of this pencil will wear out. Is that what causes fear? Or the death of the world of becoming, gaining, achieving? That world has no validity; it's the world of make-believe, of escape. The fact, the what is, and the what should be are two entirely different things. The what should be involves time and distance, sorrow and fear. Death of these leaves only the fact, the what is. There is no future to what is; thought, which breeds time, cannot operate on the fact; thought cannot change the fact, it can only escape from it and when all the urge to escape is dead, then the fact undergoes a tremendous mutation. But there must be death to thought, which is time. When time as thought is not, then is there the fact, the what is? When there is destruction of time, as thought, there's no movement in any direction, no space to cover, there's only the stillness of emptiness. This is total destruction of time as yesterday, today, and tomorrow, as the memory of continuity, of becoming.

Then being is timeless, only the active present, but that present is not of time. It is attention without the frontiers of thought and the borders of feeling. Words are used to communicate and words, symbols, have no significance in themselves whatsoever. Life is always the active present; time always belongs to the past and so to the future. And death to time is life in the present. It is this life that is immortal, not the life in consciousness. Time is thought in consciousness and consciousness is held within its frame. There is always fear and sorrow within the network of thought and feeling. The ending of sorrow is the ending of time.

## September 23

It was hot and rather oppressive, even in the gardens; it had been so hot for so long, which was unusual. A good rain and cool weather will be pleasant. In the gardens they were watering the grass and in spite of the heat and lack of rain the grass was bright and sparkling and the flowers were splendid; there were some trees in flower, out of season, for winter will be here soon. Pigeons were all over the place, shyly avoiding the children and some of the children were chasing them for fun and the pigeons knew it. The sun was red in a dull, heavy sky; there was no colour except in the flowers and in the grass. The river was opaque and indolent.

Meditation at that hour was freedom and it was like entering into an unknown world of beauty and quietness; it is a world without image, symbol or word, without waves of memory. Love was the death of every minute and each death was the renewing of love. It was not attachment, it had no roots; it flowered without cause and it was a flame that burned away the borders, the carefully built fences of consciousness. It was beauty beyond thought and feeling; it was not put together on canvas, in words or in marble. Meditation was joy and with it came a benediction.

It's very odd how each one craves power, the power of money, position, capacity, knowledge. In gaining power, there's conflict, confusion, and sorrow. The hermit and the politician, the housewife and the scientist are seeking it. They will kill and destroy one another to get it. The ascetics, through self-denial, control, suppression, gain that power; the politician, by his word, capacity, cleverness, derives that power; the domination of the wife over the husband and he over her feel this power; the priest who has assumed, who has taken upon himself the responsibility of his god, knows this power. Everyone seeks this power or wants to be associated with divine or worldly power. Power breeds authority and with it comes conflict, confusion, and sorrow. Authority corrupts him that has it and those that are near it or seeking it. The power of the priest and the housewife, of the leader and the efficient organizer, of the saint and the local politician is evil; the more power the greater the evil. It is a disease that every man catches and cherishes and worships. But with it comes always endless conflict, confusion, and sorrow. But no one will deny it, put it aside. With it go ambition and success and a ruthlessness that has been made respectable and so acceptable. Every society, temple, and church gives it its blessing and so love is perverted and destroyed. And envy is worshipped and competition is moral. But with it all comes fear, war, and sorrow, but yet no man will put these aside. To deny power, in every form, is the beginning of virtue; virtue is clarity; it wipes away conflict and sorrow. This corrupting energy, with its endless cunning activities, always brings its inevitable mischief and misery; there is no end to it; however much it is reformed and fenced in, by law or by moral convention, it will find its way out, darkly and unbidden. For it is there, hidden in the secret corners of one's thoughts and desires. It is these that must be examined and understood if there is to be no conflict, confusion, and sorrow. Each one has to do this, not through another, not through any system of reward or punishment. Each one has to be aware of the fabric of his own make-up. To see what is, is the ending of that which is.

With the complete ending of this power, with its confusion, conflict, and sorrow, each one faces what he is, a bundle of memories and deepening loneliness. The desire for power and success are an escape from this loneliness and the ashes that are memories. To go beyond, one has to see them, face them, not avoid them in any way, by condemning or through fear of what is. Fear arises only in the very act of running away from the fact, the what is. One must completely and utterly, voluntarily and easily, put aside power and success and then, in facing, seeing, being passively aware, without choice, the ashes and loneliness have a wholly different significance. To live with something is to love it, not to be attached. To live with the ashes of loneliness there must be great energy and this energy comes when there is no longer fear.

# San Francisco, 11 March 1973

A LIFE THAT is lived in fear is a dark, ugly life. Most of us are frightened in different ways, and we shall examine whether the mind can be totally free of fear. Nobody wants to be free of pleasure, but we all want to be free of fear; we don't see that both go together; they are both sustained by thought. That's why it is very important to understand thought.

We have fears, of death, of life, of the darkness, of our neighbour, fear of ourselves, fear of losing a job, insecurity, and the deeper unconscious layers of fear hidden in the recesses of the mind. Is it possible—and without analysis—for the mind to be free of fear so it is really free to enjoy life? Not to pursue pleasure, but to enjoy life? That is not possible as long as fear exists. Will analysis dispel fear? Or is analysis a form of paralysing the mind from the freedom from fear? Paralysis through analysis. Analysis is one of the intellectual forms of entertainment. Because in analysis there is the analyser and the analysed, whether the analyser is a professional or you are the analyser. When there is analysis, there is division between the analyser and the analysed and hence conflict. And in analysis you need time; you take days, years—giving you an opportunity to postpone taking action.

You can analyse the whole problem of violence indefinitely, seeking explanations for its cause. You can read volumes about the causes of violence. All that takes time, and meanwhile you can enjoy your violence. Analysis implies division and post-ponement of action, and therefore analysis brings more conflict, not less. And analysis implies time. A mind that observes the truth of this is free of analysis and therefore is capable of directly dealing with violence, which is 'what is'. If you observe violence in yourself, violence brought about through fear, through insecurity, through the sense of loneliness, dependency, the cutting off of your pleasures and so on, if you are aware of that, observe it totally, without analysis, then you have all the energy that has been dissipated through analysis to go beyond 'what is'.

How can the deep-rooted fears given to us by the society in which we live, inherited from the past, all be exposed so that the mind is totally, completely free of this terrible thing? Will it come about through analysis of dreams? We can see clearly the absurdity of analysis. And through dreams will you be free of violence?

Why should you dream at all, though the professionals say that you must dream, otherwise you go mad. Why should you dream? When the mind is constantly active both during the day and at night, it has no rest, it doesn't acquire a new quality of freshness. It is only when the mind is completely quiet, asleep, utterly still, that it renews itself. Is analysis of dreams another of those fallacies that we accept so easily? Dreams are the continuation of our daily activity through sleep, but you bring about order during the day—not order according to a blueprint, or according to the establishment of society, or according to the religious sanctions; that is not order, that is conformity. Where there is conformity, obedience, there is no order. Order comes only when you observe how disorderly your own life is during the waking hours. Through the observation of disorder, order comes. And when you have such order in daily life, then dreams become totally unnecessary.

So can one observe the totality of fear, the very root of it, its cause, or only the branches of it? Can the mind observe, be aware of, give total attention to, fear, whether it is hidden, deep in the mind, or in its daily outward expressions—like the fear of the pain of yesterday coming back again today, or coming back again tomorrow, or the fear of losing a job, of being insecure, outwardly as well as inwardly, the ultimate fear of death. There are so many forms of fear. Should we cut away each branch or tackle, come to grips with, the totality of fear? Is the mind capable of observing fear totally? We are used to dealing with fear by fragments and we are concerned with the fragments and not with the totality of fear. To observe the totality of fear is to give complete attention when any fear arises. You can invite it if you want to, and look at your fear completely, wholly, not as an observer looking at fear.

You know, we look at anger, jealousy, envy, fear, or pleasure as an observer. We want to get rid of fear, or pursue pleasure. So there is always an observer, a see-er, a thinker, so we look at fear as though we were outside looking in. Now can you observe fear without the observer? Just stick to that question: Can you observe fear without the observer? The observer is the past. The observer recognizes the reaction that it calls fear in terms of the past; he names it as fear. So he is always looking from the past at the present and so there is a division between the observer and the observed. So can you observe fear without the reaction to that as the past, which is the observer?

Have I explained it, or not? Look, if you have insulted me or flattered me, all that is the accumulated memory, which is the past. And the past is the observer, is the thinker. And if I look at you with the eyes of the past, I don't look at you afresh. So I never see you properly, I only see you with the eyes that have already been corrupted, that have already been dulled. So can you observe fear without the past? That means not name the fear, not use the word *fear* at all, but just observe?

When you observe totally—and that totality of attention is only possible when there is no observer, which is the past— then the whole content of consciousness as fear is dissipated.

There is fear from outside and fear from within. Fear of my son getting killed in a war. War is external, the invention of technology that has developed such monstrous instruments of destruction. And inwardly I cling to my son, I love him, and I have educated him to conform to the society in which he lives, which says kill. And so I accept fear, both inwardly and the destructive thing called war, which is going to kill my son. And I call that love for my son! That is fear. We have built a society that is so corrupt, that is so immoral; it is only concerned with possessing more and more, consumerism. It is not concerned with the total development of the world, of human beings.

You know, we have no compassion. We have a great deal of knowledge, a great deal of experience. We can do extraordinary things medically, technologically, scientifically, but we have no compassion whatsoever. Compassion means passion for all human beings and animals, nature. And how can there be compassion when there is fear, when the mind is constantly pursuing pleasure? You want to control fear, to put it under ground and you also want compassion. You want it all. You can't have it. You can have compassion only when fear is not. And that is why it is so important to understand fear in our relationship. And that fear can be totally uprooted when you can observe the reaction without naming it. The very naming of it is the projection of the past. So thought sustains and pursues pleasure, and thought also gives strength to fear—I am afraid of what might happen tomorrow; I am afraid of losing a job; I am afraid of time as death.

So thought is responsible for fear. And we live in thought. Our daily activity is based on thought. So what place has thought in human relationship? If it has a place, then relationship is a routine, a mechanical, daily, meaningless pleasure and fear.

# Saanen 31 July 1974

*Krishnamurti:* If I am a serious man, I want to find out why there are so many conscious as well as unconscious fears. I ask myself why there is this fear, what is the central factor of it? I am trying to show how to investigate. My mind says, I know I am afraid—I am afraid of water, darkness; I am afraid of some person; I am afraid, having told a lie, of being discovered; I want to be tall, beautiful, and I am not, so I am afraid. I am investigating. So I have many fears. I know there are deep fears that I have not even looked at, and there are superficial fears. Now I want to find out about both the hidden and open fears. I want to find out how they exist, how they come into being, what the root of them is.

Now how does one find out? I am going step-by-step into this. How does one find out? I can only find out if the mind sees that to live in fear is not only neurotic, but very, very destructive. The mind must see first that it is neurotic and that therefore neurotic activity will go on and be destructive. And see that a mind that is frightened is never honest, that a mind that is frightened will invent any experience, anything to hold on to. So I must first see clearly and wholly that as long as there is fear there must be misery.

Now, do you see that? That is the first requisite. That is the first truth: As long as there is fear there is darkness, and whatever I do in that darkness is still darkness, is still confusion. Do I see that very clearly, wholly, not partially?

*Questioner:* One accepts it.

*K:* There is no acceptance, sir. Do you accept that you live in darkness? All right, accept it and live in it. Wherever you go you are carrying the darkness, so live in the darkness. Be satisfied with it.

*Q:* There is a higher state.

*K:* A higher state of darkness?

*Q:* From darkness to light.

*K:* You see, again this contradiction. Darkness to light is a contradiction. No sir, please. I am trying to investigate, and you are trying to prevent my showing it to you.

*Q:* It is analysis.

*K:* It is not through analysis. Please sir, do listen to what the poor chap has to say. He says, I know, I am aware, I am conscious, that I have many fears, hidden and superficial, physical and psychological. And I know also that as long as I live within that area there must be confusion. And do what I will I cannot clear that confusion until there is freedom from fear. That is obvious. Now that is very clear. Then I say to myself, I see the truth that as long as there is fear I must live in darkness—I may call it light, think I'll go beyond it, but I still carry on that fear.

Now the next step—not analysis, observation only—is the mind capable of examining? Is my mind capable of examination, observation? Let's stick to observation. Realizing that as long as fear exists there must be darkness, is my mind capable of observing what that fear is, and the depth of that fear? Now, what does it mean to observe? Can I observe the whole movement of fear, or only part of it? Can the mind observe the whole nature, structure, function, and movement of fear, the whole of it, not just bits of it? By the whole, I mean not wanting to go beyond fear, be-cause then I have a direction, I have a motive. Where there is a motive, there is a direction, so I cannot possibly see the whole. And I cannot possibly observe the whole if there is any kind of desire to go beyond, or to rationalize.

Can I observe without any movement of thought? Do lis-ten to this. If I observe fear through the movement of thought, then it is partial, it is obscured, it is not clear. So can I observe this fear, all of it, without the movement of thought? Don't jump. We are just observing. We are not analysing, we are just observing this extraordinarily complicated map of fear. If you have any direction when you look at the map of fear, you are only looking at it par-tially. That's clear. When you want to go beyond fear, you are not looking at the map. So can you look at the map of fear without any movement of thought? Don't answer, take time.

That means, can thought end when I am observing? When the mind is observing can thought be silent? Then you will ask me, how is thought to be silent. Right? That's a wrong ques-tion. My concern now is to observe, and that observation is pre-vented when there is any movement, or flutter, of thought, any wave of thought. So my attention—please listen to this—my at-tention is given totally to the map and therefore thought doesn't enter into it. When I am looking at you completely, nothing out-side exists. You understand?

So can I look at this map of fear without a wave of thought?

# *From* Last Talks at Saanen 1985
## 14 July 1985

FROM CHILDHOOD WE are hurt. There is always the pressure, always the sense of being rewarded and punished. You say something to me that I get angry about and that hurts me—right? So we have realized a very simple fact that from childhood we are hurt, and for the rest of our life we carry that hurt—afraid of being hurt further, or attempting not to be hurt, which is another form of resistance. So, are we aware of these hurts and of therefore creating a barrier round ourselves, the barrier of fear? Can we go into this question of fear? Shall we? Not for my pleasure, for it is you I am talking about. Can we go into it very, very deeply and see why human beings, which is all of us, have put up with fear for thousands of years? We see the consequences of fear—fear of not being rewarded, fear of being a failure, fear of your weakness, fear of your own feeling that you must come to a certain point and not being able to. Are you interested in going into this problem? It means going into it completely to the very end, not just saying, 'Sorry, that is too difficult'. Nothing is too difficult if you want to do it. The word *difficult* prevents you from further action. But if you can put away that word then we can go into this very, very complex problem.

First, why do we put up with it? If you have a car that goes wrong, you go to the nearest garage, if you can, and then the machinery is put right and you go on. Is it that there is no one we can go to who will help us to have no fear? You understand the question? Do we want help from somebody to be free of fear—from psychologists, psychotherapists, psychiatrists, or the priest, or the guru who says, 'Surrender everything to me, including your money, then you will be perfectly all right'? We do this. You may laugh, you may be amused, but we are doing this all the time inwardly.

Do we want help? Prayer is a form of help; asking to be free from fear is a form of help. The speaker telling you how to be free of fear is a form of help. But he is not going to tell you how, because we are walking together, we are giving energy to discover for ourselves the causation of fear. If you see something very clearly, then you don't have to decide, or choose, or ask for help—you act—right? Do we see clearly the whole structure, the inward nature of fear? You have been afraid and the memory of it comes back and says that is fear.

So let's go into this carefully—not the speaker going into it and then you agreeing, or disagreeing, but you yourself taking the journey with the speaker, not verbally or intellectually, but delving, probing, investigating. We are finding out; we want to delve as you dig in the garden or to find water. You dig deep, you don't stand outside on the earth and say, 'I must have water'. You dig or go to the river. So first of all, let's be very clear: Do you want help in order to be free of fear? If you want help then you are responsible for establishing an authority, a leader, a priest. So one must ask oneself before we go into this question of fear, whether you want help. Of course you go to a doctor if you have pain, or a headache, or some kind of disease. He knows much more about your organic nature so he tells you what to do. We are not talking about that kind of help. We are talking about whether you need help, somebody to instruct you, to lead you, and to say, 'Do this, do that, day after day, and you will be free of fear'. The speaker is not helping you. That is one thing certain, because you have dozens of helpers, from the great religious leaders—God forbid!—to the lowest, the poor psychologist round the corner. So let us be very clear between ourselves that the speaker doesn't want to help you in any way psychologically. Would you kindly accept that? Honestly accept it? Don't say yes; it is very difficult. In all your life you have sought help in various directions, though some say, 'No, I don't want help'. It requires not only outward perception to see what the demand for help has done to humanity. You ask for help only when you are confused, when you don't know what to do, when you are uncertain. But when you see things clearly—see, observe, perceive, not only externally, but much more inwardly—when you see things very, very clearly you don't want any help; there it is. And from that comes action. Are we together in this? Let's repeat this if you don't mind. The speaker is not telling you how. Never ask that question how, for then there is always somebody giving you a rope. The speaker is not helping you in any way, but together we are walking along the same road, perhaps not at the same speed. Set your own speed and we will walk together.

What is the cause of fear? Go slowly, please. Cause—if you can discover the cause then you can do something about it, you can change the cause, right? If a doctor tells the speaker he has cancer—which he hasn't—but suppose he tells me that and says, 'I can remove it easily and you will be all right'. I go to him. He removes it and the cause comes to an end. So the cause can always be changed, rooted out. If you have a headache you can find the cause of it; you may be eating wrongly, or smoking, or drinking too much. Either you stop your drinking, smoking, and all the rest, or you take a pill to stop it. The pill then becomes the effect, which stops for the moment the causation, right? So cause and effect can always be changed, immediately or you take time over it. If you take time over it, then during that interval other factors enter into it. So you never change the effect, you continue with the cause. Are we together in this? So what is the cause of fear? Why haven't we gone into it? Why do we tolerate it, knowing the effect of fear, the consequences of fear? If you are not at all afraid psychologically, have no fear at all, you would have no gods, you would have no symbols to worship, no personalities to adore.

Then you are psychologically, extraordinarily free. Fear also makes one shrink, apprehensive, wanting to escape from it, and therefore the escape becomes more important than the fear. Are you following? So we are going to go over it together to find out what the cause of fear is—the root cause of it. And if we discover it for ourselves, then it is over. If you see the causation, or many causes, then that very perception ends the cause. Are you listening to me, the speaker, to explain the causation? Or have you never even asked such a question? I have borne fear, as has my father, my grandfather, the whole race in which I am born, the whole community; the whole structure of gods and rituals is based on fear and the desire to achieve some extraordinary state.

So, let us go into this. We are not talking about the various forms of fear—fear of darkness, fear of one's husband, wife, fear of society, fear of dying, and so on. It is like a tree that has many, many branches, many flowers, many fruits, but we are talking about the very root of that tree. The root of it—not your particular form of fear. You can trace your particular form to the very root. So we are asking: Are we concerned with our fears, or with the whole fear? With the whole tree, not just one branch of it? Because unless you understand how the tree lives, the water it requires, the depth of the soil, and so on, merely trimming the branches won't do anything; we must go to the very root of fear.

So what is the root of fear? Don't wait for me to answer. I am not your leader, I am not your helper, I am not your guru—thank God! We are together, as two brothers, and the speaker means it, it is not just words. As two good friends who have known each other from the beginning of time, walking along the same path, at the same speed, looking at everything that is around you and in you, so together we will go into it together. Otherwise it becomes just words, and at the end you will say, 'Really, what am I to do with my fear?'

Fear is very complex. It is a tremendous reaction. If you are aware of it, it is a shock, not only biologically, organically, but also a shock to the brain. The brain has a capacity, as one discovers,

not from what others say, to remain healthy in spite of a shock. I
don't know all about it, but the very shock invites its own protec-
tion. If you go into it yourself, you will see. So fear is a shock—
momentarily, or continuing in different forms, with different
expressions, in different ways. So we are going to the very, very,
very root of it. To understand the very root of it, we must understand time, right? Time as yesterday, time as today, time as tomorrow. I remember something I have done, of which I am shy, or
nervous, or apprehensive, or fearful; I remember all that and it
continues to the future. I have been angry, jealous, envious—that
is the past. I am still envious, slightly modified; I am fairly gener-
ous about things, but envy goes on. This whole process is time,
isn't it?

What do you consider time is? By the clock, sunrise, sunset, the evening star, the new moon with the full moon coming a
fortnight later? What is time to you? Time to learn a skill? Time to
learn a language? Time to write a letter? Time to go to your house
from here? All that is time as distance, right? I have to go from
here to there. That is a distance covered by time. But time is also
inward, psychological: I am this, I must become that. Becoming
that is called evolution. Evolution means from the seed to the
tree. And also I am ignorant but I will learn. I don't know, but I
will know. Give me time to be free of violence. You are following
all this? Give me time. Give me a few days, a month, or a year,
and I will be free of it. So we live by time—not only going to the
office every day from nine to five, God forbid, but also time to become something. Look, you understand all this? Right? Time, the
movement of time? I have been afraid of you and I remember that
fear; that fear is still there and I will be afraid of you tomorrow. I
hope not, but if I don't do something very drastic about it I will be
afraid of you tomorrow. So we live by time. Please, let's be clear
about this. We live by time, which is, I am living, I will die. I will
postpone death as long as possible; I am living and I am going to
do everything to avoid death, though it is inevitable. So psychologically as well as biologically we live by time.

Is time a factor of fear? Please inquire. Time—that is, I have told a lie, I don't want you to know; but you are very smart, you look at me and say, 'You have told a lie'. 'No, no, I have not'— I protect myself instantly because I am afraid of your finding out that I am a liar. I am afraid because of something I have done, that I don't like you to know. Which is what? Thought, isn't it? I have done something that I remember, and that remembrance says, be careful, don't let him discover that you told a lie, because you have got a good reputation as an honest man, so protect yourself. So, thinking and time are together. There is no division between thought and time. Please be clear on this matter, otherwise you will get rather confused later. The causation of fear, the root of it, is time/thought.

Are we clear that time, that is, the past, with all the things that one has done, and thought, whether pleasant or unpleasant, especially if it is unpleasant, is the root of fear? This is an obvious fact, a very simple verbal fact. But to go behind the word and see the truth of this, you will inevitably ask: How is thought to stop? It is a natural question, no? If thought creates fear, which is so obvious, then how am I to stop thinking? 'Please help me to stop my thinking'. I would be an ass to ask such a question but I am asking it. How am I to stop thinking? Is that possible? Go on, sir, investigate, don't let me go on. Thinking. We live by thinking. Everything we do is through thought. We went into that carefully the other day. We won't waste time going into the cause, the beginning of thinking, how it comes—experience, knowledge, which is always limited, memory, and then thought. I am just briefly repeating it.

So, is it possible to stop thinking? Is it possible not to chatter all day long, to give the brain a rest, though it has its own rhythm, the blood going up to it, its own activity? Its own, not the activity imposed by thought—you understand?

May the speaker point out that that is a wrong question. Who is it that stops thinking? It is still thought, isn't it? When I say, 'If I could only stop thinking then I would have no fear', who is it that wishes to stop thought? It is still thought, isn't it, because it wants something else?

So, what will you do? Any movement of thought, to be other than what it is, is still thinking. I am greedy, but I must not be greedy—it is still thinking. Thinking has put together all the paraphernalia, all that business that goes on in churches. Like this tent, it has been carefully put together by thought. Apparently thought is the very root of our existence. So we are asking a very serious question, seeing what thought has done, invented the most extraordinary things, the computer, the warships, the missiles, the atom bomb, surgery, medicine, and also the things it has made man do, go to the moon, and so on. Thought is the very root of fear. Do we see that? Not how to end thought, but see actually that thinking is the root of fear, which is time? Seeing, not the words, but actually seeing. When you have severe pain, the pain is not different from you and you act instantly, right? So do you see as clearly as you see the clock, the speaker, and your friend sitting beside you, that thought is the causation of fear? Please don't ask: 'How am I to see?' The moment you ask how, someone is willing to help you, then you become their slave. But if you yourself see that thought/time are really the root of fear, it doesn't need deliberation or a decision. A scorpion is poisonous, a snake is poisonous—at the very perception of them you act.

So one asks, why don't we see? Why don't we see that one of the causes of war is nationalities? Why don't we see that one may be called a Muslim, and another a Christian—why do we fight over names, over propaganda? Do we see it, or just memorize or think about it? You understand, sirs, that your consciousness is the rest of mankind. Mankind, like you and others, goes through every form of difficulty, pain, travail, anxiety, loneliness, depression, sorrow, pleasure—every human being goes through this—every human being all over the world. So our consciousness, our being, is the entire humanity. This is so. How unwilling we are to accept such a simple fact, because we are so accustomed to individuality—I, me first. But if you see that your consciousness is shared by all other human beings living on this marvellous earth, then your whole way of living changes. Argument, persuasion, pressure, propaganda, are all terribly useless because it is you who must see this thing for yourself.

So, can we, each of us, who are the rest of mankind, who are mankind, look at a very simple fact? Observe, see, that the causation of fear is thought/time? Then the very perception is action. And from that you don't rely on anybody. See it very clearly. Then you are a free person.

# Sources and Acknowledgments

From the recording of the public talk in Bombay, 3 January 1982, copyright © 1982/1995 Krishnamurti Foundation Trust, Ltd.

From the recording of the public talk at Ojai, 8 May 1982, copyright © 1982/1995 Krishnamurti Foundation Trust, Ltd.

From chapter 5 of *Freedom from the Known*, copyright © 1969 Krishnamurti Foundation Trust, Ltd.

From the report of the public talk at Saanen, 22 July 1965, in volume XV, *The Collected Works of J. Krishnamurti*, copyright © 1992 The Krishnamurti Foundation of America.

From the report of the public talk at Saanen, 21 July 1964, in volume XIV, *The Collected Works of J. Krishnamurti*, copyright © 1992 The Krishnamurti Foundation of America.

From *The Impossible Question*, the dialogue at Saanen, 3 August 1970, copyright © 1972 Krishnamurti Foundation Trust, Ltd.

From *The Impossible Question*, the dialogue at Saanen, 2 August 1970, copyright © 1972 Krishnamurti Foundation Trust, Ltd.

From the recording of the public talk at Saanen, 25 July 1972, copyright © 1972/1995 Krishnamurti Foundation Trust, Ltd.

From the report of the public talk at Saanen, 2 August 1962, in volume XIII, *The Collected Works of J. Krishnamurti*, copyright © 1992 The Krishnamurti Foundation of America.

From the report of the public dialogue in Rome, 7 April 1966, in volume XVI, *The Collected Works of J. Krishnamurti*, copyright © 1992 The Krishnamurti Foundation of America.

From the report of the talk with students at Rajghat School, Varanasi, 5 January 1954, in volume VIII, *The Collected Works of J. Krishnamurti*, copyright © 1991 The Krishnamurti Foundation of America.